D1459541

ONE WEEK LOAN

- 6 DEC 2005

Practising
Safe Hypnosis
A Risk Management Guide

Roger Hambleton

Crown House Publishing
www.crownhouse.co.uk

First published by

Crown House Publishing Ltd
Crown Buildings, Bancyfelin, Carmarthen, Wales, SA33 5ND, UK
www.crownhouse.co.uk

and

Crown House Publishing Ltd
P.O. Box 2223, Williston, VT 05495-2223, USA
www.CHPUS.com

British Library Cataloguing-in-Publication Data
A catalogue entry for this book is available
from the British Library.

ISBN 1899836942

Library of Congress Control Number 2002116570

Printed and bound in the UK by
The Cromwell Press
Trowbridge
Wiltshire

Dedication

I dedicate this book to my very patient and
most understanding wife, Jane.

Table of Contents

Introduction

When studying hypnosis as an alternative form of medicine I was interested in finding out if there were any risks involved in its use. I could find no single book, or other document, comprehensively covering the numerous risks and the associated adverse psychological effects.

This book collects together journal articles and extracts from books, concerned with hypnotic settings, relating to the risks and adverse psychological effects that can arise from hypnosis.

By bringing together these writings, and presenting them in a readily understandable and readable form, five distinct categories of risk have been identified. Each category examines a different aspect and attempts to cover the whole spectrum of risk.

The second part of the book addresses the laws of criminal and civil assault, and the law of negligence, as they apply to both transient and serious psychological effects – otherwise called injuries – caused by, or arising from the induction of a hypnotic trance, or the application of other hypnotic procedures.

Using my legal background and knowledge of psychology and hypnosis knowledge I have quantified the total liability of the hypnotiser at both criminal and civil law. At the same time I advise practitioners how to avoid some adverse effects by the application of good practice management.

Hypnotic adverse effects range from a headache and dizziness to anxiety and depression. Whilst the former do not qualify as injury within the meaning of an illegal assault or negligence, the latter most certainly do. In Chapter 4 a benchmark has been adopted to ascertain what qualifies as psychological injury. Without such an injury there cannot be an assault, or act of negligence, and therefore some considerable time is spent upon examining the many and varied injuries, which are directly associated with the dangers of hypnosis.

Psychological injury is often expressed to be occasioned to the 'mind'. Throughout this book Arthur S. Reber's (1995, 460) definition of the mind, from his Dictionary of Psychology, is adopted as being equivalent to the brain. Even though Reber points out that little is known about the brain, the definition '[...] must be in the final analysis be true'.

There are three principal areas for the use of hypnosis:

(1) in the laboratory setting for research and experimentation;
(2) in a clinical setting as a therapeutic medium; and
(3) upon the stage and television for the amusement of an audience.

In addition there is the amateur setting which usually consists of students experimenting with hypnosis for fun. Each of these settings is investigated in this book with reference to injuries that might result from hypnosis. Before doing so it is necessary to explore the history and theories of hypnosis from which the reader will acquire a better understanding of some of the key elements of this book.

The book starts in the eighteenth century with Franz Mesmer and his 'animal magnetism' and follows the development in hypnotism to the present day. Hypnotherapy is rapidly becoming accepted as complementary to traditional medical therapies, with many medical practitioners recommending it to their patients.

The nature of hypnosis is enigmatic, and poorly understood. Much dispute surrounds the theories of hypnosis. The nature of hypnosis is the subject of lengthy discussion: is it an altered state of consciousness, or not a separate state at all.

I have included typical methods of induction, deepeners and termination of a trance, together with explanations of attendant hypnotic jargon. It is appropriate to explain what is meant by the susceptibility of a person to hypnosis and, in addition, to describe the many symptoms of a hypnotic trance at its various levels. Such levels vary from a light hypnotic trance, experienced by everyone about ten times a day (e.g. daydreaming), to the somnambulistic level, which is a suitable depth of trance for surgery.

I know of no cases of criminal and civil assault where it has been alleged that injury was caused by, or is associated with hypnosis (the well known case of *Gates v McKenna* [1998], is based upon negligence and not assault). In the absence of legal precedent, part of the book is devoted to the elements of both types of assault and then application to injury caused by hypnosis. It is a similar situation in respect of the law of negligence, which for pragmatic reasons is considered separately from illegal assault. The results were very different to what was anticipated, particularly at the level of accountability of the hypnotiser, in both the criminal and civil laws of assault and the law of negligence.

Next, I discuss the validity of some of the different forms of consent available to persons in respect of the infliction of injury upon themselves and the application to hypnosis. I go on to mention 'informed consent', extremely important to the medical profession.

The application of the law relating to hypnosis and criminal and civil assault, the tort of negligence and consent provides a perspective upon which all hypnotisers may rely in respect of their total potential liability at English law. Thereafter, the potential liability is extended to a comparative study of American and Australian law.

It is frequently pointed out to the reader where liability to a criminal prosecution, or payment of compensation, can be incurred. However, in accordance with the main theme of this book – a risk management guide – hypnotisers are often advised how these liabilities can be avoided.

The final chapter contains a brief summary of the main themes discussed in the book.

In the UK there is a very active British Society of Medical and Dental Hypnosis (born out of an amalgamation and reconstruction of two associations in 1968) and the British Society of Experimental and Clinical Hypnosis which was founded by a group of psychologists in 1978. There is also the International Society of Hypnosis and the European Society of Hypnosis, which is proof enough that medical hypnosis has clearly advanced since the days of animal magnetism. The same can also be said of the other main area of the use of hypnosis, that is for the purposes of entertainment, with stage shows now being widely broadcast on the television.

Chapter 1

History and Theories
of Hypnosis

History

Doctor David Waxman, author of numerous articles and books on hypnotherapy, psychiatrist and founder member of The Medical and Dental Hypnosis section of the Royal Society of Medicine informs us:

> From the beginnings of the human race, man has endeavoured to impose his will and strength upon his fellow for good or for evil. From the dawn of history, with the use of witchcraft or of wizardry, of revelation through supernatural agencies, with the power of the word or the use of suggestion, he has sought to influence the destiny of others. From the accidental discovery of a natural phenomenon, through magical powers and magnetic fluids have emerged the refined techniques of the twentieth century, which produce the state known as hypnosis (1981, 1).

Some people believe that the miracles, particularly the 'cures', depicted in the Bible, can be explained by hypnotic abilities of the miracle worker. Although there is no scientific proof that any early form of hypnosis was involved, the accounts of miracle healings point towards an understanding that body and mind are interrelated in some way. An early example of Waxman's 'power of the word', perhaps.

The influence of mind over body was an important part of therapeutic 'sleep temples' of ancient Greece and Egypt. Participants were 'hypnotised' during their sleep whilst given curative suggestions. Ceremony and mysticism were important parts of the proceedings, adding weight to the visitors' belief that cures could be found within the temples.

Michael Heap, a clinical psychologist and Secretary of The British Society of Experimental and Clinical Hypnosis, informs us that:

> It is possible to make comparisons between modern hypnosis and the healing practices associated with the "sleep temples" of the ancient Egyptians and Greeks.

The Greek physician, Hippocrates (460–377 BC), often referred to as the 'father of medicine', was certainly aware of the interrelationship between body and mind. He maintained that the brain not only controlled the entire body, but also our feelings and emotions, as well as being the seat of disease.

Half a millennium later Galen of Pergamum (129–1999 AD) expanded upon the mind – body relationship and suggested that a heavenly, or ethereal fluid formed a bridge between the two. He believed that mental problems could cause physical ailments and *vice versa*. Galen, and many scientists and philosophers after him, concluded that if this fluid could be harnessed, the course of the disease could be influenced. Moreover, he thought that the fluid was instrumental in the transmission of light, heat and impulses in the nervous system.

In the sixteenth century a Swiss physician with the grand sounding name of Theophrastus Bombastus von Hohen-Heim (otherwise known as Paracelsus) radically changed most of the medical theories of the time. He agreed with the Greeks that heavenly bodies could affect humans and the course of disease. Soon afterwards a German, Athanasius Kircher, proposed that a natural power – 'animal magnetism' – was an integral to the successful treatment of ailments. Kircher's credibility was greatly enhanced when Sir Isaac Newton, endorsed his theory of animal magnetism.

The interrelationship between the body and the mind, through ethereal fluids, magnetic forces and heavenly bodies, was not the sole domain of European physicians and philosophers. In Africa and Asia the witch doctor, the fakir and the yogi practised their own specialised skills, involving different supernatural powers.

During the Middle Ages, the use of suggestion for healing purposes was regarded as sacrilegious to Christians. But many so-called 'miracle cures' were effected through sacred relics or shrines, allegedly endowed with special healing powers.

It may be that what we know as hypnosis today is derived from these ancient rituals and the customs of many cultures.

German scientist, Franz Anton Mesmer (1734–1815), introduced a fresh approach – 'animal magnetism'. While animal magnetism and hypnosis are two distinct processes, producing two somewhat different states, they no doubt coexisted in most cases.

Mesmer's dissertation at Vienna University (he graduated as a Doctor of Medicine in 1766) was entitled, 'The Influence of the Planets on the Human Body'. The central notion was that the gravitational attraction of the planets affected human health, because of an invisible fluid found in the body.

In 1775 Mesmer adjusted his theory and referred to it as 'animal magnetism', the invisible fluid behaved according to the laws of magnetism rather than gravity. He went on to explain that disease was the result of obstacles in the flow of invisible fluid through the body, with these obstacles capable of being broken by crises (trance states often ending in delirium or fits). The harmony of personal fluid flow was restored and the patient restored to good health.

There has been a belief that magnets had some sort of special curative power since ancient times. Mesmer's revised theory concluded with a great fascination with the mysteries of electricity, the power of lodestone and iron magnets. This may explain why he used the phrase 'animal magnetism'.

Mesmer applied his revised theory of animal magnetism by encouraging his patients to grasp an iron conducting rod connected to 'magnetised' iron filings and bottles of water. Mirrors were placed strategically around the room, and music was played to create an emotional atmosphere. Mesmer, dressed in a lilac coloured cloak, with an iron rod in his hand, made 'passes' – stroking movements – up and down the body, without touching the patient. This procedure was supposed to 'magnetise' the patient, and generate a crisis to cure the patient.

Mesmer had some success with this procedure and identified the types of disorder that were the most responsive to treatment.

In his historical review of hypnotism E. M. Thornton wrote:

> He [Mesmer] only treated diseases of the nervous system and these were only ones he undertook to cure; sufferers from other diseases he referred back to their own doctors, the magnetic fluid having less influence over those disorders (1976, 6).

Thornton related Mesmer's 'crises' to the epileptic propensity of many patients to nervous disorders. Here again the connection between mind and body is revealed and from which mesmerism can be clearly seen as a forerunner of the practice of present day hypnosis.

Later in the nineteenth century another common feature between mesmerism and hypnosis was forged, upon the discovery that a state of analgesia could be induced in a patient, even to the extent of performing pain free surgery, which otherwise would have been accompanied by severe pain.

A Royal Commission, set up by King Louis XVI in 1784, found that Mesmer's cures could only be explained by the imagination of the patient and that Mesmer possessed no real personal healing powers. The Commission's judgement was politically influenced by the medical profession who were hostile to Mesmer. Furthermore it was influenced by investigating that aspect of his work involving animal magnetism and invisible fluid, of which it could not, of course, find any evidence. If the Commission had properly looked into Mesmer's activities it would have discovered, according to Waxman in Hartland's Medical and Dental Hypnosis, that:

> The results were often both dramatic and surprising. Patients suffering from retention of urine, toothache, earache, depressing trances, temporary blindness and attacks of paralysis, who had hitherto been considered to be incurable, lost their symptoms completely (1989, 5).

Once more the connection between body and mind is apparent, with the cures being clearly effected by the influence of Mesmer upon the mind of the patient. The majority of the illnesses listed by Waxman may now be classified as psychosomatic. The remainder are associated with pain which is a topic previously mentioned as being eminently treatable by mesmerism. The main point of this observation is that mesmerism, as also with hypnosis, is a treatment initially directed at the mind, even though it is able to remedy both mental and bodily ailments.

The father of modern hypnotism was the Portuguese, Abbe de Faria, who called the hypnotic state 'lucid sleep'. He rejected the whole of the animal magnetism theory, pouring scorn on it in a series of lectures he gave in Paris in 1813.

Faria gave his subjects verbal suggestions after first inducing lucid sleep – hypnotic trance – and then invoked the phenomena of hypnosis, such as hallucinations, inhibitions and unwilled movements and post hypnotic suggestions. Unlike the Mesmerists, Faria realised that the induction of a hypnotic trance does not depend upon any special power, but almost entirely on the innate ability of the subject and the techniques of the hypnotist.

James Braid (1795–1860), a British surgeon and another pioneer of hypnosis, also separated the phenomena of hypnosis from the theories of mesmerism. He first introduced the term 'hypnosis' in his book, *Neurypnology* – or the rationale of nervous sleep considered in relation with animal magnetism – in which Braid acknowledged the role of suggestibility and imagination when he wrote:

> The oftener patients are hypnotised, from association of ideas or habits, the more susceptible they become, and in this way they are liable to be effected entirely through the imagination (1843, 36).

Whereas Mesmer gave us the word 'mesmerism', Braid gave rise to the term 'hypnotism'. However, of more importance was Braid's scientific approach to hypnosis, which with its psychological realities demonstrated that the observed phenomena are the product of imagination being highly influenced by the suggestions of the hypnotist.

Braid first experimented upon his friends and relatives and discovered a trance was easily induced by sitting them comfortably and then having them fix their eyes upon a bright object, whilst making suggestions. He used the trance state for healing purposes and also for pain free surgery.

At about the same time a British surgeon, James Esdaile, was also performing surgical operations using hypnotic anaesthesia, whilst working in a prison hospital in India. It is reported that Esdaile performed about three thousand operations, of which more than ten percent were of major surgery and using nothing but hypnosis as an anaesthetic. In his book of 1846, *Mesmerism in India and its practical application in surgery and medicine* he described how mortality generally ranged from 25–50% and that he was at the top end of that statistic, until he started using hypnosis as a form of anaesthesia, when the rate dropped to 5%. The most likely reason therefore is that the subconscious mind must develop a greater resistance to infection in the body.

It was left to Viennese physician, Doctor Josef Breuer (1842–1925) to find the vital clue in order to extend the use of hypnosis into a more valuable and wider field, in that he pioneered its use for the treatment of hysteria. In this context hysteria describes a condition where the most frequent symptoms are: hallucinations, somnambulism, functional anaesthesia, functional paralysis and dissociation, which are, of course, all psychiatric disorders.

Breuer accidentally found that one of his female patients spontaneously spoke about her problems while under hypnosis, but in a profoundly emotional manner, and when returned to a fully conscious state her symptoms had disappeared. This emotional reaction caused Breuer – and his friend, Sigmund Freud – to conclude that symptoms could be removed if their apparent cause is eliminated. This was a great step forward in hypnotic therapy.

Sigmund Freud (1856–1939) continued to work with Breuer and their collaboration produced some of the most famous written case histories, entitled *Fraulein Anna O'*. Anna O' suffered from a squint, persistent cough, various paralyses and visions of black snakes. Under hypnosis she regressed, with accompanying emotional reactions. Freud called these reactions a 'catharsis', which he regarded as a purging of problems repressed below the level of conscious awareness.

During his work with Anna, Freud was developing and formulating other ideas, including dream interpretation, and he decided to abandon the use of hypnosis entirely to pursue his new method known as free association. This abandonment effectively blocked the progress of hypnotherapy for nearly fifty years. It has been suggested that Freud chose to pursue other avenues because he was not a very good hypnotist. This might have been because of his cancer of the jaw and rendering him unable to speak in the manner required of a hypnotiser.

It was not until the First World War that hypnotherapy was again revived. It was used for both symptom removal and repressed traumatic experiences. Once again, hypnosis was found valuable in the therapeutic relief of symptoms by 'reliving' the traumatic experiences that originally produced them, during a hypnotic trance.

In the years following the First World War, hypnosis again fell into a decline. Behaviourism and psychoanalysis were in vogue, with only a small number of medical and dental personnel maintaining a practical interest. However, 'Misuse by charlatans, entertainers and lay therapists, claiming the cure of an extensive variety of ailments by direct symptom removal' thrived, according to Waxman (1989, p. 15).

One notable exception to the post WW1 hypnotherapeutic drought was Clark Hull who published a book in 1933, about experimental and theoretical contributions to the subject of hypnotherapy, called Hypnosis and Suggestibility. He wrote, about the decline in hypnosis,

> [...] The century since 1825 has shown a remarkable sterility: Almost nothing has been accomplished during this period except the very gradual correction of [...] errors. (1933, p. 18).

About half a century after Freud abandoned hypnosis, another psychotherapeutic technique was introduced – an effective treatment known as 'desensitisation'.

Nevertheless, there was, and there continues to be, one aspect of hypnotherapy that is deficient, in that there is still no organised teaching of hypnosis in the UK, which has been largely by private enterprise. In 1955 the British Medical Association recommended that a description of hypnosis and of its psychotherapeutic possibilities, limitations and dangers be given to medical under-graduates and instruction in its clinical use be given to certain postgraduate trainees. Despite this recommendation a study by D. L. Scott (1978, p. 13) found that of thirty two medical schools and eighteen dental schools in Britain only two of each provided some very limited undergraduate training. Only these two medical schools, but no dental schools, provided some official, but equally limited postgraduate lectures.

Nevertheless advances in the knowledge about the hypnotic state, from laboratory experimentation and the exploration of neuro-physiology of hypnosis and the advancement in hypnotherapeutic techniques of treatment continues unabated.

Nowadays medical treatment by hypnosis is generally accepted, by both the medical profession and the general public, as a branch of alternative medicine. Many General Medical Practitioners often refer patients to hypnotherapists when traditional methods of treatment are having little or no success. It is becoming increas-ingly common for hospital doctors to rely upon hypnotic anaes-thesia in surgery and for babies to be delivered while their mothers are under hypnosis. This is in addition to frequent use in dental surgeries. Routine use of hypnosis in Europe, America and Australasia is increasing, with interest also being shown in South Africa and Japan.

Theories

There are six main theories. The first – the Suggestion Theory – is preferred among hypnotists, including me, and as a result it is dis-cussed at greater length than the others.

The Suggestion Theory

Doctor Ambroise August Liebeault is the first recorded user of hypnosis to suggest that it could be induced by a specific condition of enhanced suggestibility, delivered by verbal suggestion. Freud did not believe that suggestion was capable of definition. However, Heap has recently provided a most acceptable definition as follows:

> A suggestion may be defined as a communication conveyed verbally by the hypnotist the purpose of which is to direct the subject's imagination in such a way as to elicit intended alterations in the way he or she is behaving, thinking or feeling. (1996, p. 498).

It should be noted that suggestions are accepted by subjects without a logical reason for doing so. This is one of the main bases of the treatment of ailments by hypnotherapy and, of course, hypnotic stage and television shows.

The term 'suggestibility' should be distinguished from suggestion. Suggestibility is the extent or measure to which a person is inclined to uncritically accept ideas and propositions. Whereas, we are exposed on a daily basis to suggestions, whether it be advertisements on the television or articles in the press, the extent to which we are influenced is our degree of suggestibility. In hypnotic terms, some persons are more susceptible to suggestion than others.

Doctor H. B. Gibson, President of the British Society of Experimental and Clinical Hypnosis, and Doctor Michael Heap in their book *Hypnosis in Therapy*, advise that:

> All the available evidence points to the conclusion that 'susceptibility' and 'hypnotic state' are closely connected and the more suggestible the subject the more readily can hypnosis be induced and deepened. (1991, 21).

In addition, Chemnitz and Feingold linked the two elements of suggestion and suggestibility when they described suggestion as:

> [...] A stimulus which induces suggestible behaviour and experience. Suggestible behaviour and experience are described as emotional, uncontrolled, uncritical and often unconscious behaviour, whilst suggestibility is understood as the tendency to react to suggestions and therefore means a personality trait. (1980, p. 76).

In his book, *The Structure of Human Personality* (1970), Hans J. Eysenck, the eminent German born British psychologist advises us that personality traits are 'relatively enduring' and therefore a person's degree of suggestibility could remain fairly static during his or her lifetime. Heap confirms this: 'It appears that suggestibility is a very stable characteristic which tends to remain relatively stable throughout a person's lifetime.' (1996, p. 499).

Heap advises that the other central process, related to suggestion, is the trance being: '[...] A waking state in which the subject's attention is detached from his or her immediate environment such as feelings, cognition and imagery.' (1996, p. 498). This trance state is similar to daydreaming – an average person experiences this at least ten times daily – absorption in a book or even watching the television. (A detailed examination of the induction, maintenance and application of allied procedures of a hypnotic trance follows in the next chapter and the nature of hypnosis in Chapter 4.)

Why are suggestions in the hypnotic state – even sometimes in a light hypnotic trance – readily acceptable and actioned, even when the same suggestions would be first critically assessed, and perhaps rejected, in the fully conscious state?

First, we must accept the concept of the unconscious mind (otherwise often called the subconscious mind) as first proposed by Sigmund Freud. One aspect of the unconscious mind is that we are unaware of its presence and also of its contents, even though it constantly influences our thoughts and behaviour.

Even though the unconscious is able to exercise most of the functions of the conscious mind, it cannot critically evaluate situations. Therefore a person in a fully conscious state being asked to perform a silly function, such as eating an onion in the belief it was an apple, would critically evaluate the suggestion and reject it. However, in an hypnotic state the same person would eat the onion thinking it was an apple. The difference is that the unconscious mind makes the decision to uncritically accept the suggestion and not reject it. Thus the power of criticism, according to Ivan Pavlov (who is mentioned again shortly) and many others after him, the power of criticism is either fully or partially suspended when a person is in an hypnotic trance.

A suspension of the power of criticism may explain why people are ready to accept suggestions which become embedded in the subconscious. Thereby the suggestions assume reality and are acted upon.

The more the conscious mind is suppressed the more the suggestibility of a person will increase. When an hypnotic trance is induced, the deeper the trance the greater the exposure of the unconscious mind and the less active the conscious mind becomes. If very deep hypnosis or somnambulism is achieved, it seems that the unconscious mind is in complete control and the power of criticism is removed altogether. A client receiving therapeutic treatment unquestioningly accepts the suggestions under hypnosis and post-hypnotically the unconscious mind automatically respects those suggestions. There can be great ameliorative effect upon say, tension and anxiety, when the unconscious mind acts upon suggestions of calmness and peace and they are treated by the conscious mind as real and are acted upon.

Gibson and Heap, writing about certain principles applicable to the hypnotic state:

1.   The response to hypnosis will depend upon the extent to which the power of criticism is suppressed and the power of rejection normally exercised by the conscious mind is removed.

2.   The depth of hypnosis in any given case will be directly related to the degree of suppression attained. Slight suppression will result in light hypnosis only: complete suppression will result in deep hypnosis or somnambulism. moved.

3.   The more the conscious mind is suppressed, the more the suggestibility of the individual will increase. (1991, pp. 23–4).

The Pavlovian Theory

This theory is also known as 'Conditioned Response' and was first proposed by the Russian psychologist Ivan Petrovic Pavlov (1849–1936) who is best known for his experimentation with animals. He maintained that responses to stimuli in humans and animals are learned and form habits. He called these habits 'conditioned responses'.

Pavlov proposed that hypnosis produced conditioned responses. He thought that the hypnotic suggestions made by the hypnotist produced changes in the workings of the mind. He believed that the civilising and critical parts of the brain become inhibited under hypnosis, while the more primitive parts that are more susceptible to suggestion become dominant. Pavlov went on to theorise that if suggestions were repeated when the primitive parts were dominant, a conditioned response would be created and this response would be hypnotic in nature.

Putting his theory into practice Pavlov showed how a particular response could be produced by the same stimulus being applied, time and time again. He demonstrated that a particular word or gesture could induce a hypnotic trance in a subject. This is how a hypnotist on the television prepares his subjects beforehand, so that he is able to whisper a word, or tap them on the shoulder, to induce an immediate trance, saving on transmission time. It must be pointed out that such hypnotists, on both stage and television, only select and use the most susceptible subjects.

Likewise a hypnotherapy client being treated for anxiety and tension, is conditioned under hypnosis to react to the word 'calm' by suggesting that the use of this word will produce calmness and relaxation, when in a fully conscious state. Thereafter the client will think of this word when he or she becomes anxious or tense, and even though in a fully conscious state, will become relaxed and calm. I have used this method and found it most successful.

Even though Pavlov proposed this theory of hypnosis he still maintained that hypnosis is a form of sleep. This cannot be the case because it has been demonstrated by many other people that hypnosis and sleep are two different physiological states. (These 'states' are discussed at some length in Chapter Four.) Furthermore whilst a person is in sleep there is a loss of consciousness, but in a hypnotic trance, whilst there is a degree of loss of awareness, there is no loss of consciousness. In addition it cannot be a form of sleep because in hypnosis there is a knee jerk reaction, but not such a reaction whilst in sleep and, in the latter state, the subject would not hear any of the suggestions or instructions given by the hypnotist.

The final words on the Pavlovian Theory are from Waxman:

> There is no doubt that in hypnosis, conditioning take place: conditioning to close the eyes at a certain signal, conditioning to achieve complete physical relaxation, conditioning to allow mental calm, and conditioning to respond to certain other signals in a specific manner […]. (1981, p. 24).

The Psychoanalytical Theory

There are many psychoanalytical techniques aimed at releasing information from the unconscious mind, where it is sheltered by stratagems that Freud named 'defence mechanisms'. These defence mechanisms are designed to deal directly with feelings of anxiety, rather than with the source, hiding the anxiety from the conscious mind.

According to Freud, the release of repressed information causes a catharsis, because the information is no longer prevented from reaching consciousness, or otherwise disguised. Whatever defence mechanism is employed, and no matter the nature of the material in the unconscious mind, the protection from external reality is removed by the release of the material into the conscious mind. It is at this stage that the catharsis occurs with its consequential and subsequent beneficial effects.

One of the cornerstones of the theory is the concept of the unconscious mind. It is an important concept in hypnotherapy generally, including psychoanalytical hypnotherapy, since a fundamental premise of hypnosis is the existence of the unconscious mind. The fact that the therapist is in direct touch with the unconscious mind is a distinct advantage over nonhypnotic psychoanalysis.

Hypnosis as Dissociation

This theory is based on the idea that hypnosis abolishes volition and is a form of automatism. The theory was first proposed by the French philosopher, author and Professor at the College de France, Pierre Janet (1859–1947), who extensively studied hysteria and hypnosis. Hysteria is described in the Oxford Medical Dictionary as 'formerly, a neurosis characterised by [...] repression, dissociation [...] and vulnerability to suggestion.' (1998, p. 322). There is a close association between hysteria and hypnosis, repression and suggestion.

Janet concluded that hysteria was caused by splitting the conscious mind into two parts, which resulted in the unconscious mind becoming the dominant part. This splitting of the mind in hysteria

13

was the same as the processes at work in hypnosis. The idea of splitting of the mind entered into psychiatric medicine under the name of 'dissociation' which is defined in the Oxford Medical Dictionary as 'the process whereby thoughts and ideas can be split off from consciousness and may function independently [...]' (1998, p. 189).

The dissociation theory is acceptable in accounting for the nature and phenomena of hypnosis but it fails because of its dependence upon the occurrence of amnesia. This dependence arises from failure to recall information, caused by a break in the associated chain of information. When this situation arises it creates a state of amnesia, and thereby dissociation. Thus, amnesia is an essential element in the theory, but this is where the theory loses some credibility, in that even deep trances can occur without any great loss of memory of events, both before and during hypnosis. As a result it must not be thought that the theory is substantially discredited, because posthypnotic amnesia can occur if it is suggested to the subject that he or she will experience loss of memory in respect of certain specified events. This tends to support the dissociation theory even though not arising naturally.

The American experimental psychologist Ernest R. Hilgard thought that posthypnotic phenomena could form part of Janet's theory of hypnosis as a dissociation. Hilgard stated:

> Some cognitive systems, even though not represented in consciousness at the time, continue to register and process incoming information and when such a system is released from inhibition it uses this information as though it had been the conscious all along. (1978, 124)

Hypnosis as Role-playing and Goal-directed Fantasy

Doctors T. X. Barber and Nicholas P. Spanos
Barber maintains that the subject of a hypnotic trance tries hard to play the role of an hypnotised person, willing to carry out what he or she thinks is expected of an hypnotised person (1974, 500–11).

Spanos developed a 'goal-directed fantasy' theory. This occurs where the 'thinking and imagining with suggestions' of the subject is directed at imagining a situation in accordance with the suggestions made. If it was suggested to the hypnotised subject that an arm is so heavy that it cannot be lifted, and at the same time a heavy weight is visualised holding the arm down, then the subject would be engaged in a goal-directed fantasy.

Before Barber and Spanos, R. W. White concluded that hypnosis should be regarded as a 'goal-directed striving' whilst behaving like a hypnotised person:

> We suggest and make it clear, to the subject what we expect him to do, and because of the existing rapport he seems to strive to fulfil the role we have outlined. His dominant motive seems to be submission to the operator's demands.

In his book, *Hypnotism*, (1957), Estabrooks related that the testing of hypnotic anaesthesia with electric shocks showed subjects could withstand shocks ten times as strong as those in the fully conscious state and apparently without any additional discomfort. If the subjects were role-playing they would not, of course, submit to huge electric shocks without anaesthetic.

It is appropriate that this chapter, having started with a quotation from Waxman's Hypnosis, it should end with one from him, taken from Hartland's Medical and Dental Hypnosis:

> It would seem that our present knowledge of human behaviour is not yet sufficiently developed to produce a complete and satisfactory theory of hypnosis. In trying to define it accurately we are only describing an end result … In most trance states, suggestion, dissociation and conditioning all play a part to some extent. (1989, pp. 31–32).

Chapter 2

Induction of Hypnotic Trance

It is important to be familiar with certain terms and procedures relating to the process of hypnotism, particularly in later chapters. In addition it will also prove useful to have some knowledge of the susceptibility of a subject to hypnosis and the different levels of trance which can be attained.

This chapter explains some methods of the induction of a hypnotic trance, and how a trance is deepened. It continues with details of how a trance can be terminated. Finally, the susceptibility of a person to hypnosis is examined in greater detail as well as the symptoms of hypnosis at various levels of trance.

Induction

Before the induction of a hypnotic trance, any misconceptions or anxieties the subject may have about hypnosis, must be discussed. If this preliminary step is not taken, induction may be frustrated, because one of three essential criteria is not met.

The first criterion is that a person wants to be the subject of hypnosis. If a prospective subject does not really want to be hypnotised, it would be an almost impossible task for the hypnotiser to induce a trance.

The second criterion is that a prospective subject wishes to be hypnotised for whatever reason or purpose.

The final criterion refers to the subject not fighting against the induction of a hypnotic trance.

Another important preliminary to the induction of a hypnotic trance is to ascertain if the subject has been recently drinking alcohol or taking drugs, such as tranquillisers, because such items can combine with the hypnosis and cause an abreaction (a sudden and strong release of emotion). It should be further ascertained if there are any medical conditions from which the subject suffers as again an abreaction may be caused. For example, it would be inappropriate for a hypnotiser to interfere with the respiration and pulse rates of a subject with an adverse heart condition by altering the natural rate of breathing.

The method of induction to be employed should be explained so the subject is assured that there will be no loss of control. Furthermore it should also be explained that even though the word 'sleep' is often used, hypnosis is not a form of sleep, but a particular form of relaxation. It is hoped by this time that the person to be hypnotised is starting to relax, because this is the whole basis of the induction of a hypnotic trance and its maintenance. It should be stated that there are other methods of inducing a trance, in addition to the ones set out below, such as by a shock or by confusion, but these are so little used it is not worthwhile setting out any detail in this book.

There are two things being achieved when a person is hypnotised:

(1) the relinquishing of critical processing of all the information from without and reliance upon the hypnotiser to carry out that task; and
(2) the hypnotist's suggestions to the subject are the only source of attention to the subject.

There are a number of methods of induction because an induction to hypnosis should be tailored for the individual's needs and with experience a hypnotiser knows which method or combination of methods to use. For example it would be inappropriate to use an authoritarian method upon a retired spinster schoolteacher who was herself an authoritarian, but it would be a different matter if the subject was a serving member of H.M. Forces, used to receiving orders rather than giving them. The consequence of using an inappropriate script is, of course, that induction of a trance does not occur, no doubt, to the embarrassment of the hypnotist. It often happens that induction scripts, as well as scripts for other purposes (including therapies), are personally compiled by the hypnotist to suit the subject and the subject's circumstances. The ability to compile scripts can only be acquired with experience.

The mode of delivery of the induction script is most important and is not easy to master. It should be in a slow, boring, monotonous and monotone voice and this applies no matter what induction method is being used.

There are three induction by relaxation methods:

The Permissive Method

A good description of this method is 'eye fixation with progressive relaxation'. A typical induction script, relating to the Permissive Method, is set out in Part I of Appendix A to this book (p. 181).

It will be seen from this typical script that the whole basis of the induction of a hypnotic trance is suggestions of relaxation.

After the script is administered, in the manner mentioned earlier, the subject should be in a light hypnotic trance with eyes closed and completely relaxed. If this is not the case the hypnotist should continue with further suggestions of relaxation until the subject is ready for deepening of the trance.

The Intermediate Method

This method is reliable and quick, provided the subject is suitably prepared as described earlier in this chapter. It should take only two or three minutes to control eye closure.

It can be seen from the induction script, set out in Part II of Appendix A (see p. 182), that the Intermediate Method is the reverse of the Permissive Method because the aim is to distract the subject's mind from the induction process. This is achieved by giving the subject some kind of mental task which will fully occupy the conscious mind and thereby leaving the unconscious mind more accessible. (The division of the conscious from the unconscious mind is discussed in both Chapters 2 and 3 and in particular in relation to Freud's model of the mind and the Psychoanalytical Theory.)

While the subject is occupied with the mental task the hypnotist suggests feelings of relaxation, increased tiredness and heaviness, but the subject is instructed not to listen to these suggestions, to ignore what is being said and concentrate on the mental task. By this means the unconscious mind is open to suggestions, accepts them and they become reality.

The script is based upon Erickson's hand levitation induction method which was originally devised by Milton H. Erickson in 1923. It is one of the best induction techniques, since it not only permits subjects to play a part in the induction, but also allows them to take their own time in entering the hypnotic state.

The Authoritarian Method

Suggestions of relaxation are again made in this method, but the emphasis is on telling the subject he or she is relaxing. This is a technique which can be particularly economical in time when used by experienced hypnotists. There is a modified authoritarian script by a well-known hypnotherapist, Dave Elman, that somewhat widens the scope of its application. I often rely on this further modified form, which can be found in Part III of Appendix A (p. 185).

Deepener

A 'deepener' simply is a means to deepen a hypnotic trance. After a successful induction, when the subject's eyes have closed and a light hypnotic trance has been achieved, the next stage is to gradually deepen that trance as much as possible.

The importance of deepening a trance is that, for example, applying therapies is much easier when the subject is in a deeper trance, rather than just under light hypnosis. However, it does not mean that dozens of therapies such as, stopping smoking, slimming, confidence building and calming examination nerves, are ineffective when only in a light hypnotic trance. With other therapies, for example, alleviating anxiety and depression, curing phobias and, naturally upon the stage and television, it is most preferable to achieve a much deeper level of hypnosis.

When the dangers of hypnosis are investigated later, it will be interesting to see if greater danger is related to deeper trance.

There are many types of deepeners and two are outlined below:

Direct suggestion

During the induction procedure a factor is introduced whereby it is frequently suggested that the subject is going into a deeper and deeper state of relaxation (Authoritarian Induction Script set out in Part III of Appendix A, p. 185) where suggestions of relaxation are repeated, coupled with words such as 'deeper and deeper'. Furthermore, a post hypnotic suggestion linked with suggestions of a deeper trance can play an important part in respect of subsequent sessions of hypnosis. For example, while under hypnosis, it can be suggested to the subject: "Next time ... you will not only fall asleep more quickly ... but you will also relax into a deeper, deeper sleep ... much deeper than this time."

Use of imagery

It is no use trying to deepen a trance by employing imagery if the subject cannot visualise. A simple test of visualisation capability is always advisable before induction commences if a deepener of this nature is to be employed. A good test is to ask the subject, with eyes closed, to describe a favourite pair of shoes or boots, including the colour.

When using a deepener that includes visualisation it is important to ascertain first if the subject suffers from any medical condition which could precipitate an abreaction whilst under hypnosis. For example, if the subject suffers from hay fever, it would be totally inappropriate to have her imagine walking across a lawn, with bordering flower beds, in the summertime. The images are so real that the subject could suffer an attack of hay fever. A script to

21

deepen a trance by imagery is contained in Part IV of Appendix A (p. 187).

Termination

The complete termination of a trance is emphasised when the risks of hypnosis are discussed later in this book. In stage hypnosis, any amusing suggestions acted upon by a member of the audience, during a performance, could lead to both physical and psychological injury, if the participant is not properly brought out of a trance. One example, leading to minor physical injury only, is a member of the audience taking a bite of an onion and believing it was an apple. If the trance is not properly terminated the same person could continue to eat onions after leaving the theatre with a resultant deleterious effect on the stomach.

Major injury could result in other circumstances, such as a subject driving a car and responding to Elvis Presley music on the car radio by gyrating around and pretending to play a guitar. Psychological injury can easily result in a subject being hypnotically placed in an anxiety provoking situation, which continues after failure by the hypnotist to properly and thoroughly terminate the trance.

Some inexperienced hypnotists, both on and off the stage, only count to the number three before informing the subject that the trance is terminated. To be absolutely safe it is preferable to count to say seven and talk to the subject in between each number by reminding the subject where he or she is located, the time and date and so on. The adverse psychological effects caused by the failure to dehypnotise are discussed in some detail later (see Chapter 7). A termination script, used by me, is contained in Part V of Appendix A (see p. 187).

Susceptibility

This section on susceptibility deals with the differential susceptibility to hypnosis by different people and groups of people.

Some subjects are anxious to be hypnotised, but despite their fullest co-operation are unable to experience anything other than a very light trance – not being apparent to the subject and not perceptible even to an experienced hypnotist – if any trance at all. On the other hand some people are enormously susceptible to hypnosis and can experience a trance within the first few lines of an induction script. Evidence of this extreme susceptibility is most obvious when a stage hypnotist makes suggestions to the audience at large and some members of the audience submit to hypnosis by, for example, being unable to unclasp their hands. By this means the hypnotist entices the willing and most susceptible people on to the stage.

Ernest R. Hilgard (1965), the American experimental psychologist, informs us that relatively few people are not susceptible to hypnosis. Using the Stanford Hypnotic Susceptibility Scales (see below for description) he found that five to ten percent of the population could not be hypnotised, with only about five percent being able to achieve a deep trance.

It was originally thought by Josephine R. Hilgard (1970), an American hypnotherapeutical clinician, that people could be classified in relation to susceptibility by their personality (extrovert, introvert and so on), but after much experimentation this theory was abandoned. It is now thought that those with good imagination, who enjoy day dreaming, or can generate vivid mental pictures, are most susceptible.

Susceptibility to hypnosis stabilises upon a person reaching maturity, but the same stability is not present in children. Thus, there are separate scales of hypnotic susceptibility for adults and children. It has been long acknowledged that children are more susceptible to hypnosis than adults. Over one hundred years ago H. Bernheim, an historian on hypnosis, stated:

> As soon as they are able to understand, children are as a rule very quickly
> and easily hypnotised. (1886/1973, p. 2).

The optimum age for maximum susceptibility to hypnosis is about nine years, but after about twelve years of age it steadily declines with age until adulthood.

With regard to sex differences and susceptibility to hypnosis C. L. Hull (1933), an American psychologist, related the difference to the reliable and already quantified difference in the height between males and females. He estimated that, on average, females exceeded males in susceptibility by one fifteenth of the degree to which men are taller than women, in other words, very little. Hull was subsequently supported by many other writers and experts in the field of hypnosis, except E. R. Hilgard who denied that there existed 'any sex difference in susceptibility' (1965, 317).

Symptoms

There are many scales of hypnotic susceptibility. They are designed to measure susceptibility and do so by ascertaining the depth or level of a hypnotic trance by a combination of the observed symptoms during hypnosis and those symptoms supplied by the subject upon a debriefing after termination of a trance. Among some of the common characteristics that can be easily observed are: hypnotic mask, breathing more relaxed, reduced blood pressure, heart rate becomes slower, galvanic skin response, involuntary swallowing is increased, eyelids may flutter, lacrimation and feeling warmer.

In experimental research, some sort of measuring instrument with a scale is required that can be employed by clinicians. Many such scales have been devised for defining the depth of a trance and which list the symptoms exhibited relating to the depth or level of a trance. One system for defining the different depths of a trance is the Lecron and Bordeau system which is regarded as an extremely complete method of 'scoring'. It is summarised in Part VI of Appendix A (see p. 188).

The Lecron and Bordeau system that uses five depths or levels of trance starting with 'Hypnoidal', which is less than a light trance, and finishing with a 'plenary', in which all spontaneous activity is inhibited. It is from a plenary trance that somnambulism can be developed by a suggestion to that effect. There are fifty symptoms spread over the five levels, but a hypnotised person will not manifest all symptoms and may experience only two or three at each level. The depth of a trance is mentioned from time to time and it is useful to know that these scales exist and to be able to understand them.

Chapter 3

The Nature of Hypnosis

Defining and Characterising

In both a criminal prosecution for assault and a civil claim for damages upon the ground of assault and battery, it is always stated how, and with what, the injuries were inflicted. For example, a fist, rugby boot, rolling pin or knife. Each of these articles has a physical presence and can be produced in a court of law. However, hypnosis as an alleged instrument causing injury is intangible. As a result the nature of hypnosis has either, to be authoritatively and consensually defined, or its characteristics clearly described.

Furthermore, when considering consent to hypnosis (particularly informed consent – see Chapter 13, p. 141) it is most important to be able to explain the nature of hypnosis. The subjects being made aware of the nature of hypnosis – of which the risks form part – enables them to make a clear assessment before participation.

When a criminal prosecution, or a civil claimant, alleges psychological injury in a case of assault, precedent dictates that psychiatric evidence must be adduced as to the nature of the injury (e.g. depression, anxiety with or without panic attacks, and paranoia), (see Chapters 11 and 12). It follows that the same principle must apply where psychological injury is allegedly caused by the induction of a hypnotic trance. This would be an impossible task if a so-called expert witness was unable to define, or at least detail, the characteristics of hypnosis as the instrument causing the injury. At present, there appears to be no reported case of a criminal prosecution for assault, where it is alleged that hypnosis is the instrument occasioning injury, or in the civil courts in respect of assault and battery.

This chapter seeks to define, or in the absence of an acceptable definition, to describe the nature of hypnosis by reference to its characteristics. In the absence of a definition or description it would be impossible to prosecute hypnotisers in the criminal courts successfully, or claim against them in the civil courts.

Defining hypnosis

Hypnosis is a most complex psychological phenomenon, with no agreed definition – not even among the experts. There are even some who believe that there is no such thing as a 'hypnotic state' (e.g. Barber 1969) and refer to it instead as a 'non-state'.

It will be recalled that the preferred theory is the Suggestion Theory, which states that when a person is the subject of a hypnotic trance the conscious mind is so suppressed that the unconscious mind is exposed to suggestion, which it accepts without criticism.

Orne (1972, p. 102) relates to the Suggestion Theory when he defines hypnotic behaviour as:

> Hypnotic phenomena can only be distinguished when suggestions are given which distort his perception or memory. The hypnotised individual can be identified only by his ability to respond to suitable suggestions by appropriately altering any or all modalities of perception and memory.

When Orne wrote this definition he was researching the distinction between certain hypnotic and nonhypnotic behaviours, but it applies equally well to stage hypnosis where the modalities of perception and memory are invariably altered.

The Psychoanalytical Theory encompasses Freudian theory and is applied while the subject is under hypnosis. The definition of Gill and Brenman (1959, p. xxiii):

> [...] An induced psychological regression, issuing in the setting of a particular regressed relationship between two people, in a relatively stable state which includes a subsystem of the ego with varying degrees of control of the ego apparatuses.

The Suggestion and Psychoanalytical Theories demonstrate how different definitions can be.

Lack of consensus also relates to the applications of hypnosis in experimental and clinical settings. In experimental investigations of hypnosis attempts are made to measure the external, observable behaviour of the subject, but in the clinical setting the emphasis is upon access to subjective experiences. The settings and objectives are different, adding to the distance between the two approaches and therefore problems of definition. Experimental hypnosis is set in laboratory conditions, while therapeutic hypnosis is conducted in a clinical environment. The object of the former is to investigate the phenomena of hypnosis and the latter is to apply therapies to relieve mental and bodily ailments.

Anyone who has seen a stage, television, or private performance will realise that hypnosis employed for such purposes is most comfortably situated within the Suggestion Theory. This type of hypnosis is, of course, an application solely designed to produce extraordinary, observable and out-of-character behaviour in the participating subjects. Whilst it may suit the Suggestion Theory it is certainly not contained in the experimental and clinical approaches, in so far as setting and objective are concerned.

Scheflin and Shapiro (1989, p. 134), whose book *Trance on Trial* addresses hypnosis, criminal and civil offences and court evidence, set out the following forensically based definition of hypnosis:

> Hypnosis is an altered state of consciousness, characterised by intensified concentration of awareness on suggested themes, along with a diminished interest in competing perceptions. Subjects who are hypnotised experience perceptual and sensory distortions and enhanced abilities to utilise normally unconscious mental mechanisms.

Even though Scheflin and Shapiro (a lawyer and doctor respectively) offer this as a definition of hypnosis, only the first part 'Hypnosis is an altered state of consciousness [...]' is strictly a definition of hypnosis. The remainder merely describes some characteristics of hypnosis. They do emphasise the importance of a definition in legal procedures, where 'specification of the exact definition is crucial' (p. 126).

The final word upon defining hypnosis, or one should say lack of a consensual definition, is from James R. Hodge:

> It is a fact we don't know exactly what hypnosis is, and every definition ultimately is either vague and theoretical or is involved merely with a description of the phenomena that can be elicited by the hypnotic state. (1974, p. 126.)

I said at the beginning of this chapter, that because hypnosis was intangible, it was desirable to be able to define it in a generally acceptable manner. Clearly, this is impossible. The next best thing is to describe the nature of a hypnotic trance in terms of its characteristics.

Defining characteristics of hypnosis

It is important to understand what is meant by a 'characteristic' and to distinguish it from a symptom and a phenomenon.

Reber (1995, p. 777) defines 'symptom' as:

> [...] Any event or change in state in a system that tends to occur with another event or change of state and hence can be taken as an indicator [...] of it.

In context, 'another event or change of state' is the induction of a hypnotic trance and the 'change in state of in a system' is the symptom or 'indicator'.

'Characteristic', again according to Reber, is 'Some individualistic feature, attribute, etc. that serves to identify and 'characterize' something.'. (1995, p. 120).

The generally accepted measuring instrument for depth of hypnotic trance is the 'Lecron and Bordeau system', which specifies the symptoms and phenomena exhibited for each of the four depths of trance (see Part VI of Appendix A, p. 188). For example, two of the many symptoms to indicate a light trance are slower and deeper breathing and twitching of the mouth during induction. In a deep trance the symptoms include an ability to open the eyes without affecting the trance and a fixed stare when eyes are open, with papillary dilation. There are over fifty of these symptoms listed by Lecron and Bordeau that are, referring to Reber's above definition, symptoms which can be taken as indicators of the characteristics of hypnosis upon the induction of a trance.

'Phenomenon' differs from a characteristic of hypnosis in that the former simply means an event that may be observed. Depth of a trance can be measured using the Lecron and Bordeau system by 'symptoms and phenomena'. This means that all the symptoms may be observed by the hypnotiser and others upon the induction of a trance. In other words, this is an objective method of measurement and quantitative collection of data. In addition this is where another and important difference arises between a characteristic and symptom of hypnosis, when analysing its nature. Characteristics of hypnosis are of a subjective and therefore qualitative nature and cannot be observed symptoms and phenomena are manifest and can be observed.

Some writers use the words characteristic, symptom and phenomenon interchangeably and therefore must be interpreted carefully in the context in which they occur.

Main characteristics of hypnosis

Ask a group of experienced users of hypnosis, whether they are researchers, therapists or stage entertainers, to name five characteristics of hypnosis that most typified its nature, and each would respond differently. This would not mean any one of them was wrong, but this highlights the influence of differing theories of hypnosis. The following characteristics are influenced by the Suggestion Theory and describe the nature of hypnosis, but not in hierarchical importance.

Increased suggestibility
Suggestibility under hypnosis is increased. This enhanced imaginative capacity does not necessarily mean that a subject will comply with suggestions which would be found displeasing in the fully conscious state. However, the greater the suggestibility possessed by a person the greater the susceptibility to hypnosis. Not only is a trance easier and quicker to induce, but a deeper trance is also achievable.

Scheflin *et al* (1989, p. 124) describe the characteristic of increased suggestibility as 'The increased ability to respond positively to ideas offered by the hypnotist or by the self'.

Reality testing reduced
The subject, while in a hypnotic trance, uncritically accepts ideas and propositions suggested by the hypnotiser. The unconscious mind responds to suggestions because, unlike the conscious mind, it has no critical powers and so the conscious mind's critical or reality testing abilities are reduced.

Gibson and Heap (1991, p. 7) write of reduced reality testing:

> Subjects tend to accept ideas and even distorted perceptions of hypnosis that are presented to them without much concern for logical consistency.

When reality testing is reduced the effect is to suspend, or partially suspend, everyday logical thinking by virtue of the conscious mind becoming less functional and, at the same time, exposing the unconscious mind.

Alongside the suspension of everyday cognitive logic and thinking is the uncritical acceptance of material from the hypnotist. This includes acceptance of imaginary phenomena in place of incoming experiences through the senses. This is an ideal situation for a stage hypnotist to have a subject accept things which are contrary to his or her beliefs.

Enhanced role play
The best example of this characteristic is to suggest to the hypnotised subject that he or she returns to a much younger age, when the childhood role is played far more convincingly than normal.

To achieve this childhood state it is necessary to utilise a hypnotic technique called 'age regression' (sometimes called 'revivification'). It entails asking a deeply hypnotised adult to imagine going back in time, in place and in memory to a particular age (it is preferable to select a notable day such as Christmas or a birthday) and relive and recount some experiences involving the subject which occurred at the specified age. The subject will speak and act as a child with a most noticeable change in demeanour and a switch to the present tense. Intriguingly the subject is capable of remembering experiences and events which took place at that time, which cannot be recalled in the fully conscious state. In addition, if the subject is asked to write his or her name, the handwriting is childish and that compares well with the subject's own handwriting at the same age. The reproduced behaviour is generally regarded as being far too accurate to be a pretence.

Posthypnotic behaviour
Behaviour after termination of a trance can be affected by what has been suggested during hypnosis. For example, the hypnotist might instruct a hypnotised member of the audience that (after being dehypnotised) upon hearing the band play a particular tune, to stand up, punch the air and loudly shout "The Russians are coming". Upon hearing the musical cue this posthypnotic action is performed without conscious awareness on the part of the subject. The subject may be aware of the origins of the suggested behaviour, but the behaviour is nonetheless automatic.

A deep hypnotic trance is required to create posthypnotic behaviour. In an experiment concerning posthypnotic behaviour Orne, Sheehan and Evans (1968, p. 189) report:

> Consistent posthypnotic response outside the experimental setting was related to the level of hypnosis subject achieved at the time the posthypnotic suggestion was administered.

Orne *et al* aimed to ascertain if subjects would posthypnotically react to the word 'experiment' by touching their foreheads and also if suggestions of posthypnotic amnesia were effective. The posthypnotic suggestions were given before suggested amnesia for all trance events. Upon hearing the word 'experiment' in the ordinary course of conversation, all the subjects touched their foreheads. The subjects could not account for this behaviour, or its origins.

When suggesting posthypnotic behaviour to a hypnotised subject, it is a matter of good practice to ensure the behaviour is in response to a cue from the hypnotiser alone, or upon the hypnotiser's direction. The Orne *et al* study did not include these instructions, because a reaction was required upon the cue word being spoken by a third party. Additionally it wise to fix a time limit upon the posthypnotic behaviour. In the Orne *et al* study a 48-hour limit was set. A prudent stage hypnotist should limit the posthypnotic behaviour to the time the subject leaves the theatre.

Ideosensory activity
'Ideo' means mental image with 'ideosensory' meaning a mental image of the product of the senses. This characteristic of ideosensory activity relates to a hypnotised person's capacity to form sensory images which are different from those presented to him or her in the physical environment. The senses are being deceived or, at the very least, confused.

The images may be positive, for example: tastes (chocolate and bacon); aromas (baking bread and silage); sights (computer screen and pint of beer); and sounds (Beatles' recording and child crying). Or negative, which is the denial of a particular presence.

While ideosensory activities could be said to be of a deceptive nature, this is not the case with hallucinations as part of ideosensory activity. These hallucinations involve a perception that an object is actually present or absent. Thus, as a positive hallucination, a subject may 'see' his grandfather stood in front of him and be induced to talk to him. Or a subject may experience a negative hallucination, and be unable to 'see' a third person in the room. Positive and negative hallucinations can be manufactured by a hypnotist, but in ideosensory activity as a characteristic of the nature of hypnosis, they arise naturally and without intervention.

Details of the images can only be obtained from the subject on a self report, because they form part of subjective experiences and cannot, therefore, be used for therapeutic or other purposes.

The above main characteristics, belonging to the nature of hypnosis, appear instead of an agreed definition of hypnosis. Other characteristics include: passivity (subjects rely on the hypnotist to direct their actions); narrowing of attention (focusing only on that which the hypnotist calls to the subjects' attention); amnesia (automatic erasure of events in hypnosis); hypermnesia (greater recall of detail than when in fully conscious state); and analgesia and anaesthesia (deadening or alleviation of pain).

In the absence of an agreed definition of hypnosis, the characteristics of its nature are available and, are likely to be admissible as evidence of the presence of a hypnotic trance in a court of law.

State or Nonstate?

The so-called theories of hypnosis, are really ideas from different groups of people as to **why** a hypnotic trance arises. They are not theories in the strict sense of the word, but are perspectives or different ways of viewing the reasons why hypnotic procedures induce a trance. One example is the ever popular suggestion theory, which relies upon repeated suggestions to induce a hypnotic trance.

The first part of this chapter deals with defining and characterising hypnosis, in other words **what** is hypnosis. This part investigates **how** a hypnotic trance is formed. It is reasonable to assume that underlying mental or physical processes produce what is commonly known as a state of hypnosis. This 'state of hypnosis', otherwise regarded as 'an altered state of consciousness', and the later critical appraisal of the nonstate theory, are very important parts of the examination of the nature of hypnosis. They could be the deciding factor in the success or failure of a court case.

There are theorists who support the 'state theory' of hypnosis on the basis that it differs fundamentally from the normal waking state, but there are others, called 'nonstate' theorists, who reject the hypothesis that hypnosis is a distinct state or condition.

A state of hypnosis

For the last half century researchers have been debating how a hypnotic trance can best be described and understood as the product of an altered state of consciousness. During this time some versions of the state theory have been abandoned, to the extent that some have asked if the state debate remains the axis around which research and theory revolves. Therefore, as a preliminary, the first task is to decide whether the state theory remains a force to be reckoned with.

Kirsch and Lynn (1995) advise that the two opposing factions of state and nonstate camps – as they were referred in the 1960s and 1970s – continued into the 1980s, but with the labels changing to special process and social psychological respectively. Kirsch and Lynn write that recently:

> new theories of hypnosis have been proposed by a new generation of scholars. As a result, what was once real has become a myth. The notion of warring camps is now outdated (p. 847).

Not all would agree with this unilateral declaration of peace, particularly as there is no general consensus upon the 'new theories of hypnosis' mentioned by Kirsch and Lynn. It is interesting to note that elsewhere Lynn proposes a new theory of sociocognitive hypnosis which can be comfortably placed under the nonstate banner. In 1996, Wagstaff concluded:

> The state-nonstate controversy is still very much alive, and sides in this debate seem to be as far apart as ever. (p. 20).

Without question psychologists continue to be divided upon whether hypnosis produces a trance-like altered state of consciousness.

The American Psychological Association (APA) Division of Psychological Hypnosis defined hypnosis as a procedure wherein changes in sensations, perceptions, thoughts, feelings, or behaviour are suggested. A number of well known and respected scholars were involved in the drafting of this 'definition', which strongly implies that hypnosis is an altered state of consciousness. Whilst this may be an appropriate description for the purposes of the APA, it is neither specific nor sufficiently pragmatic for this book.

Kirsch, Mobayed, Council and Kenny (1992) identified four specific premises shared by state theorists:

State theorists' first premise
'Hypnotic inductions produce altered states of consciousness in susceptible persons.' This premise is ambiguous and could mean a hypnotic trance is only available to people who are susceptible, or that different people are susceptible to varying depths of trance. In fact, according to Hilgard (1965) there is only about 5% of the general population who are not susceptible. Of the 95% remainder of the population who are susceptible to hypnosis in varying degrees, perhaps the top 5% are highly susceptible and can be found, for example, amongst those members of a stage hypnotist's audience who enter a trance without even leaving their seats and, as a result, finish up on the stage.

What the state theorists are really relying upon are the symptoms, produced by the induction of a trance in susceptible persons, as evidence of an altered state of consciousness.

Second premise
'These hypnotic states are introspectively distinguishable from waking consciousness and from other altered states (e.g. sleep or intoxication).' Introspective reports, being a report of the examination of one's mental experiences (the contents of one's consciousness) are generally regarded as being fairly reliable as a qualitative method for the collection of data. In fact, introspective self-reporting is the only method available to state theorists in seeking support for their theory, because covert mental activity is obviously not directly observable. Even though there are outward signs or symptoms of a trance in hypnotised persons, they cannot be used to interpret internally experiences of an altered state of consciousness.

However, there is one objective method to test for an altered state of consciousness (i.e. a state of hypnosis) and that is to measure the change, if any, from the normal waking state in the brain waves of a hypnotised person using an electroencephalograph. It is worth noting that the premises contained in Kirsch *et al* do not take into account this means of testing.

Third premise

'[…] Persons are more responsive to suggestion in hypnotic states than in nonhypnotic states.' This premise adopts a 'cause and effect' stance in that it maintains the hypnotic state is the causal explanation for the increased responsiveness to suggestions from the hypnotiser. Hilgard (1986) accepted that there must be a connection between responsiveness in subjects and the hypnotic state:

> […] Produce enough changes for the subject to identify that some massive changes have taken place (if he is hypnotically responsive), and these changes have a common influence on responsiveness to suggestion (p. 167).

Here again, the subject is left to report the inner changes taking place from the waking state into the hypnotised state.

The fourth premise

'Heightened suggestibility is not the only characteristic of hypnotic states.'

Other discussed characteristics included enhanced role play, reality testing reduced and ideosensory activity, amnesia, narrowing of attention, analgesia and anaesthesia with all these characteristics supporting this 'state theorists' premise.

A nonstate of hypnosis

Many experts have written about the state and nonstate perspectives of hypnosis. One Such is John E. Chaves, who writes of the nonstate perspective:

> […] Hypnosis is not productively viewed as a special state […] and instead sees hypnotic phenomena as the product of comparatively mundane cognitive and social variables that have become relatively well understood, coupled with a view of the hypnotic participant as acting strategically to have the experiences and exhibit the behaviours that are suggested […] (1997, p. 252).

What Chaves is not so simply stating is that some factors operate to produce trance-like behaviours, but this does not amount to a state of hypnosis as maintained by the state theorists. In 1973, William C. Coe wrote:

> The nonstate position holds that hypnotic behavior may be examined and explained by concepts that are applicable to other behavioral patterns, and that seeking an elusive altered state of consciousness is not a fruitful endeavor. (p. 118)

Coe reviews five of the experimental approaches which were employed in hypnosis research and revolved around the state-nonstate issue. Upon analysing these experimental approaches he found sympathy with the nonstate view.

Nearly twenty years later, Coe (1992) was still of the same mind, but wrote more forcefully: '[...] There are no researchers who seriously postulate a special state or a trance as a causal variable [...]' (p. 118).

Once again Kirsch *et al* (1992), provide three bases upon which the nonstate theorists rely, to show that state theory is without foundation. The nonstate theorists do not set out to directly prove the nonstate perspective, but critically attack the state perspective.

The first nonstate basis
[...] No physiological markers of the hypothesized state have been found [...]

In the latter part of the nineteenth century it was discovered that electrical impulses emanated from the brain, but it was not until 1928 that Hans Berger invented the electroencephalograph (EEG) which measured these impulses by affixing electrodes to the scalp. The impulses were recorded as waves on a graph and in due course the machine became sufficiently sophisticated to distinguish between the impulses produced during the waking state and sleep. There are five EEG changes occurring in sleep, including drowsiness, a relaxed rhythm, and three stages of sleep. The first stage, known as alpha rhythms, appears in people when they are relaxed, with eyes closed and in a quiet place.

Experimentation using an EEG reveals the alpha rhythms show little change in frequency between that of a hypnotised person and someone who is physically relaxed. Typical of this type of physiological experiment is that reported by Waxman (1981) which is contained in papers donated to the British Society of Medical and Dental Hypnosis by Professor Barry Wyke, a neurological scientist. Wyke stated, *inter alia,* that the brain waves are similar in a hypnotised person to that produced if the same person were awake but relaxed.

The nonstate theorists claim that EEG experiments clearly show that hypnosis does not affect the brain, or other physical system, and so it is not a special state of altered consciousness.

An interesting aspect of these EEG hypnotic experiments is the conclusion that the induction of a hypnotic trance does not induce sleep, but the subject continues in in a waking state. Waxman (1981, p. 34) states that brain waves only change '[...] When sleep is deliberately and specifically induced by the hypnotist.'. The subject may not, of course, be as alert as before induction, but it is obvious a subject is clearly in a waking state.

Sometimes hypnotists talk of inducing a sleep in subjects and in some induction scripts the subject is told to "Go to sleep", (see Chapter 2 and Appendix A, Parts I, II, and III (pp. 181–6)). This reference to sleep is clearly inaccurate, because hypnosis resembles sleep to an observer only.

The second basis
[...] All of the phenomena produced by suggestion after a hypnotic induction can also be produced without a hypnotic induction.

The nonstate perspective has sometimes been misunderstood, and simply interpreted as a hypnotised subject complying with the hypnotist's suggestions – in the sense of faking. However, this is not so. The nonstate theorists recognise that, faking apart, the subject undergoes genuine changes in experiences produced by suggestion. The Meeker and Barber (1971) study is a good example. It is concerned with, among other things, '[...] The high base rate of "waking" suggestibility [...]' (p. 61).

Meeker and Barber based their journal article on both temporary experimental research in hypnosis, and observations of professional stage hypnotists, publications regarding stage hypnosis and their own personal experience and training in stage hypnosis. They set out a number of basic principles which underlie stage hypnosis, including:

> Base level or "waking" responsiveness to suggestions is much higher than is commonly assumed.

According to Meeker and Barber it has been well known for some time, in the stage hypnotists' profession, that a hypnotic trance is not necessary to obtain responsiveness to suggestions from on stage volunteers. 'The *Encyclopedia of Stage Hypnosis* states unequivocally that "it is possible to produce very striking hypnotic effects in the waking state, entirely independent of the trance [McGill, 1947, p. 28]".'

McGill (1996, p. 294) provides a reason why he believes some people simulate being hypnotised:

> [...] Simulation is not necessarily voluntary deception, but is frequently born of a desire to cooperate with the performer and help the show. In other words, not being able to enter into true somnambulism the subject does his best to initiate the condition.

Meeker and Barber (1971, p. 70) again:

> Although laymen seem to believe the stage performer is a highly effective hypnotist who places his subjects in a hypnotic trance, a more valid conception is that the stage performer is an actor playing the role of a hypnotist.

McGill (1966) states the subjects initiate the hypnotic role play, but Meeker and Barber (1971) place the onus upon the performer, playing the role of an hypnotist, as a result of which the subjects respond to his suggestions. The difference is of no practical consequence. The important point is their agreement that hypnotic phenomena can be produced without a hypnotic induction.

Even though the nonstate theory is here restricted to stage hypnosis, it applies to other settings. Barber (1969, 100) was one of the first researchers to suggest and present:

> A formulation [...] which does not invoke a special state of consciousness ("hypnosis" or "trance") to account for the behaviors that have been historically associated with the word hypnotism Barber based his study upon detailed examination of several dozen experimental studies and concluded that the so-called hypnotic state was determinable by antecedent variables, such as, the '[...] Subject's attitude, expectancies and motivations with respect to the situation [...]' (p. 100).

Barber provides examples of behaviours related to this nonstate, determined by antecedent variables, of analgesia, hallucination, age regression and amnesia. It is noteworthy that these behaviours are included as characteristics of hypnosis earlier in this chapter.

The third basis
The increases in suggestibility that are produced by hypnotic induction are small [...] and can be duplicated or even surpassed by a variety of other procedures including [...] imagination training [...]

Kirsch *et al* (1992) provide experimental data for this nonstate basis. Their study involved sixty students, divided into four separate groups. The first group was subjected to traditional hypnotic induction. The second group was given a modified version of the hypnotic induction of the first group, where all references to relaxation, sleepiness and heaviness were substituted with suggestions for increased alertness, energy and lightness. The third group received relaxation training including instructions to tense and relax various sets of muscles in turn. The fourth group was given instructions upon how to use goal-directed fantasy to produce hypnotic responses. This last group was told it could produce hypnotic experiences by thinking and imagining along with suggestions given by the experimenter.

The subjects produced self-reports of both their state of awareness and experiences during each of the four procedures, with twenty four of the reports being analysed by 18 experts in the field of hypnosis. The very interesting results are summarised as follows:

Experts findings of subjects' open-ended reports indicated that

> *(a) traditional hypnotic inductions produce a state of consciousness that is indistinguishable from nonhypnotic relaxation training;*

(b) *the subjective experience of hypnotic suggestions after imagination training is indistinguishable from that after hypnotic inductions; and*

(c) *suggestibility is unrelated to state of consciousness as assessed by experts.*

Kirsch *et al* offer these results as evidence that tends to support the nonstate theorists.

The examination of the nonstate theory involved both objective (EEG testing) and subjective (self-reports) methodology, but the state theorists were restricted to the use of introspection only.

The nonstate theorists' view can be summarised as hypnotic experiences that are produced by a person's beliefs and expectations and not by an altered state of consciousness.

An important point to be made at the end of this examination of both state and nonstate theories is that the characteristics of hypnosis remain the same whatever side of the debate one supports. The debate, therefore, has no effect upon the value of court evidence of the existence of a hypnotic trance, discussed at the beginning of this chapter. However it could have an effect upon the matter of consent to the induction of a trance, which is a topic examined later (see Chapter 12).

Chapter 4

Risks – an Overview

There are a number of approaches to the risks associated with hypnosis. Each approach or perspective needs to be considered in terms of illegal assault, because any perceived injury arising could form part of an assault in criminal or civil law. At civil law an assault, where injury is caused, is technically called 'a battery', but unless the strict meaning is otherwise required, it will remain an assault for the purpose of this Guide.

What constitutes an assault is discussed later (See Chapter 10 on criminal assault and Chapter 11 on civil assault). In the meantime this chapter is concerned with the nature of psychological injury which needs to be inflicted upon a victim to complete a criminal offence, or incur civil liability. Usually in criminal law it can be generally stated that the more severe the injury, the greater and more serious the offence. In civil law the more severe the injury, the greater the liability – usually financial – upon the offender. This means that, first of all, an injury has to be inflicted, which is recognised as such in law, and then its severity has to be assessed in order to gauge the extent of the responsibility, if any, of the person causing the injury.

Psychological injury or harm has long been recognised as satisfying the definition of injury as a part of an assault. It follows that psychological injury (called 'after', 'adverse', or 'negative' effects, 'complications' and 'unusual reactions' in hypnosis terms) arising from the induction of a hypnotic trance must also satisfy the definition. If any of the risks are realised and result in injury, the question of whether these injuries are as a result of an assault on the mind is debated in the chapters concerned with both assault and consent. Therefore, this book is not only concerned with the dangers, but also with injuries arising from them.

The Nature of Psychological Injury in Assault

The nature of an injury can determine whether an illegal assault has taken place and is, therefore, an essential factor when discussing both the dangers of hypnosis and, more particularly, any associated adverse effects.

Litigation, arising from the adverse effects of hypnosis, is so rare that there are no legal precedents with which to draw a scale of injuries or to consult when deciding if a particular injury properly forms part of an illegal assault. However, based on criminal prosecution in respect of three of the four statutory assaults, it has been held that psychological injury or harm means that very thing, provided it is not of a minor or temporary nature. It has also been held that evidence of psychological injury must be given by a properly qualified psychologist or psychiatrist. This means that mere emotion – which is a term explained later in this chapter – and most everyday common complaints, such as a headache and other complaints of a minor nature, are excepted and do not count as injury for the purpose of criminal assault. The same principles would apply to injury at civil law, upon the basis of *de minimus non curat*, which means that the law does not concern itself with very small matters.

The nature of the injury must be sufficient to qualify as a constituent part of an assault, otherwise the assault is negated. Therefore, the problem is how to decide whether or not a particular psychological injury qualifies as an integral part of an assault while, at the same time, being acceptable in law.

DSM-IV

It can be argued that there is a simple answer to the problem of deciding whether a psychological injury qualifies as part of an assault and that is to adopt what is commonly referred to as the DSM-IV, as a benchmark. Its full title is the Diagnostic and Statistical Manual of Mental Disorders (4th revision of 1994) and it is the official system for classification of psychological and psychiatric disorders prepared and published by the American Psychiatric Association (1994). The DSM-IV is one of two systems currently in use – the other is the ICD-10 (mental disorders section of the International Classification of Diseases, 10th revision 1993). When DSM-I was first published in 1952 there were only about one hundred listed disorders, but the latest edition, DSM-IV, contains in excess of 300.

Both systems are regarded as being 'complete' medical models but the DSM-IV is the preferred system. However, with greater European integration ICD-10 (being an international system as opposed to DSM-IV which is American) could become the specified form of classification of mental disorders. DSM-IV has 17 major categories and ICD-10 has only 11 but, there are no real differences between the two. In any event both systems incorporate a catch-all category which caters for any deficiencies in the listed disorders, as well as any new disorders which may become accepted by mental health professionals from time to time. Therefore, if ICD-10 is adopted there will be a common basis in the European Union, but the language of mental disorders will remain the same elsewhere.

DSM-IV assumes that the origin of abnormal behaviour lies in a malfunction of the body or brain and further assumes that different types of malfunctions will produce different types of mental illnesses. It is these illnesses or disorders, that can allegedly arise from the induction of a hypnotic trance, and attendant procedures, which are are central to this book. (The words 'illness' and 'disorder', which are used both in this risk management guide and in quotations from books and journals, have gradually become to mean the same thing.)

DSM-IV is frequently referred to throughout this book. It is mainly used for the purpose of ascertaining if certain medical or mental conditions are listed, where it is alleged they have been occasioned by the induction and maintenance of a hypnotic trance. For convenience, completeness, and the use of the reader, the major categories in DSM-IV (together with explanations of such categories) are set out in Part I of Appendix B (see p. 191).

Some of the disorders contained in DSM-IV are highly unlikely to be associated with hypnotic dangers. For example, organic diseases (neurological rather than psychological), such as Alzheimer's.

Before the adoption of DSM-IV, most adverse psychological and psychiatric conditions were mainly divided between two categories, of neuroses and psychoses. Quotations in this book often refer to these two categories and therefore it is important for the reader to understand a little about them. A neurosis, according to Reber (1995, p. 491), is 'a personality or mental disturbance due to any known neurological or organic dysfunction, i.e. a psychoneurosis'. (Neurological means related to the central nervous system). Reber's definition is used to describe symptoms of neuroses and, aetiologically, to indicate the cause or origin of the production of the symptoms. To resolve anxiety there are defence mechanisms which can be raised, with them ultimately producing the observed symptoms. Examples of neuroses include, anxiety, phobic, obsessive compulsive, depressive and narcissistic.

Reber also provides a definition of psychotic disorder: 'A general cover term for a number of severe mental disorders of organic or emotional origin.' (p. 622). Reber refers to 'emotional origin' in his psychosis definition. The 'emotion' – historically defying consensual definition – involved in this definition is somewhat different to the 'mere emotion' mentioned on page 65: a 'mere' emotion is an adverse effect being of a minor nature and therefore not qualifying as an injury for the purpose of illegal assault. It is accompanied, for example, by fear, joy, disquiet, unhappiness and love, and is relatively short-lived. However, in some cases the emotional state is inappropriately chronic and can lead to psychotic disorders. Psychotic disorder symptoms include, delusions, hallucinations, dramatically inappropriate moods and incoherent speech.

The adoption of DSM-IV, has not made the terms neurosis and psychosis redundant, far from it, they are still deeply entrenched in psychological language. Other categories, less common than neuroses and psychoses, include personality disorder and subnormality. These latter categories are, of course, also included in DSM-IV.

MacHovec's list of complications

At this stage it is appropriate to examine a definition of the adverse effects of hypnosis, or 'complications' as Frank J. MacHovec, labels them:

Hypnosis complications are unexpected, unwanted thoughts, feelings or behaviors during or after hypnosis which are inconsistent with agreed goals and interfere with the hypnotic process by impairing mental function. There is no prior incidence or history of similar mental or physical symptoms. They are nontherapeutic (would not form part of a treatment plan or research protocol) or antitherapeutic (treatable conditions of and by themselves). (1986, p. 16.)

This is a far reaching definition and includes all adverse effects, of whatever nature or duration, and no matter how mild or severe they may be.

In another journal article MacHovec (1988, p. 46) comprehensively lists the 'complications' associated with hypnosis. The list is based on published clinical and experimental research, as well as MacHovec's own experience of hypnosis over eighteen years of clinical practice. He refers to the list and writes, '[...] Many complications coincident with hypnosis have been reported in persons with no prior medical or psychiatric history of them or similar symptoms' (p. 45). This means that 'pre-existing conditions' are not present, as far as one can ascertain, when the subject is hypnotised and therefore it is reasonably safe to assume that the complications have been caused by hypnosis.

MacHovec's summary list of complications associated with hypnosis is set out in Part II of Appendix B (p. 193).

Some of MacHovec's complications, are emphasised in italics to indicate that they are contained in DSM-IV (see Appendix B, Part I (p. 191)) and satisfy this practice guide's definition of illegal assault. Some of these emphasised complications are included in DSM-IV disorders although not actually named in the DSM-IV list. For example, MacHovec's 'body/self-image distortions' are part of 'depersonalisation disorder' (under the main heading of Dissociative disorders). In addition some symptoms of disorders listed by MacHovec, such as 'tremor' form part of Anxiety disorders in DSM-IV.

Injuries of a minor nature do not qualify as part of an illegal assault and that is the case with many of MacHovec's listed complications. Relevant to all injuries, of whatever nature, is MacHovec's useful definition of what he calls the 'intensity' of the complications:

Intensity varies from mild, moderate to severe: from uncomfortable, annoying, transient symptoms which fade with or without treatment (mild), to those persisting with significant anxiety or agitation and disrupt the subject's everyday living (moderate), to totally disabling or life-threatening medical or psychiatric emergencies (severe). (p. 46).

It is those complications of a moderate and severe intensity in which could form injuries and part of an illegal assault. In addition to injuries of a minor nature those of a transient nature also do not qualify as an injury as part of an illegal assault. MacHovec is again helpful in respect of the duration of complications when he states that they are either, '[...] *Acute* (short-term), lasting hours to weeks, or *chronic* (long-term), lasting months to years' (p. 46).

However, each case has to judged upon its facts. In some studies, where there is little or no indication of an adverse effect, assumptions have to be made and are sometimes influenced by the nature of the adverse effect. For example, ordinary everyday depression, from which we all suffer from time to time, is obviously mild and short-term, whereas a personality disorder (called a 'personality change' in the MacHovec list) is certainly moderate, if not severe, in intensity and is undoubtedly long-term.

Using MacHovec's definitions, the 'injury' element of an 'illegal assault' can be described as an injury of psychological origin which is caused by hypnosis, contained in DSM-IV and is of neither a minor nor temporary nature.

It must be emphasised that even though some after effects of hypnosis (for example, headache, dizziness and nausea) are embraced by the above MacHovec definition, and not listed in DSM-IV, it does not mean that they are not real and unpleasant. It merely means that they do not satisfy the injury element of an illegal assault. This is the value of having the benefit of a benchmark such as DSM-IV where psychological injury is consistently defined, and also one has the certain knowledge that the listed disorders are recognised in law as being acceptable psychological injuries, within the legal meaning of assault.

After Effects not Coincident with the Use of Hypnosis

Adverse effects – which translate in this book as 'injuries' – have so far been assumed to have been caused by the induction of a hypnotic trance, or by the subsequent procedures. However, this is not always the case. A subject may have a pre-existing condition, either physical or mental.

This umbrella term of 'pre-existing condition' covers a number of situations, which are recognised by Drs Louis West and Gordon H. Deckert, both of whom practised and carried out research in American hospitals and universities. In a 1965 journal article they comprehensively set out the circumstances of risks to the subject from pre-existing conditions.

It would be unfair if hypnosis alone was blamed as the proximate cause for adverse effects of a hypnotic trance, when a medical or mental disorder was pre-existing and the hypnosis, for example, reacted adversely with it.

Pre-existing conditions are an extremely important aspect in determining whether injury has been 'caused' by hypnosis. The studies cited in this book have been carefully monitored by qualified medical personnel. Nonetheless even the most experienced psychiatrist would sometimes have difficulty in categorically stating that a particular individual was not, say, a latent schizophrenic, and the hypnosis was not sufficient to precipitate something that was inevitable.

It should be mentioned that pre-existing conditions are rightfully classified as 'risks of hypnosis' because of the adverse reactions that can arise. However, only after effects which constitute 'injury' (within the meaning of 'assault' and DSM-IV) and are caused by hypnosis, that are of interest in this guide.

Those risks related to pre-existing conditions include the following:

Risk of precipitating a mental disorder

A disorder, such as schizophrenia, may be in its infancy where some symptoms have started to form, with the disorder thereby not being complete and apparent, but is precipitated by hypnosis.

Illustrative of this situation is the recent High Court case of *Gates v McKenna* when the very well known stage and television hypnotist Paul McKenna was sued for damages by Christopher Gates, who suffered an acute schizophrenic episode the day after stage hypnosis and was admitted to hospital. He became of a permanent schizoid personality for which he said McKenna was responsible. However, the court held that 'common sense' suggested Gates' condition had reached the stage at which the disease could easily have been triggered by hypnosis, but not caused by it. This is the only reported case where alleged psychological injury has been attributed to hypnosis.

Another example of the precipitation of a mental disorder by hypnosis is reported by Rosen (1960, p. 686). An adolescent was hypnotically cured of a wry neck and as a result was able to cancel his hospital appointment for surgery. The hypnosis involved age regression when he relived a sexually traumatic episode. Afterwards he became an 'exhibitionist' and a practising homosexual.

Risk of making an existing disorder worse

An existing disorder being worsened is one of the most likely effects following the employment of hypnosis. Some of these after effects can be serious disorders in their own right, listed in DSM-IV and amounting to injury within the meaning of an illegal assault. Moreover, in the treatment of some ailments a subject may react as though the induction of a trance is a sort of threat to a symptom and upon finding this threat most disturbing a more serious condition may result.

Examples of these more serious conditions are related by Drs H. Rosen and L. H. Bartemeier (1961), both psychiatrists in American teaching hospitals. They report on a patient who was hypnotically 'cured' of numbness in an arm but, afterwards, developed an acute schizoid psychosis.

Meldman (1960, p. 361) recognises symptom substitution and advises that 'hypnosis is effective for symptom removal'. However, he continues with a warning:

> Symptom removal can be hazardous, however, and should not be used when the symptom is related to an obsessive–compulsive system or to a serious personality, character, or ego defect.

Before DSM-IV most adverse mental conditions were divided between neuroses and psychoses – much to the chagrin of the psychology student who had to learn the differences – of which schizophrenia comprised both conditions. Attempts to treat the neurotic components (e.g. anxiety) of schizophrenia sometimes fail and result in increased intensity of symptoms. According to West and Deckert (1965, p. 95) one reason for this is the subject's increased anxiety about, and upon, being hypnotised.

However, it cannot be said that the increase in the intensity of say, schizophrenic symptoms are injuries caused by hypnosis, but it could be argued that the increase in intensity is additional or further injury to that which existed before hypnosis.

It has also been reported that some depressed subjects have been known to become suicidal after hypnosis. Rosen (1960, 686) dramatically tells of the patient who suffered from severe back pain that disappeared post hypnotically. About a week later the patient committed suicide by jumping out of an upper window. Rosen advises that pain can be wholly or partially emotionally based and frequently masks severe and even suicidal depression.

Risk of prolonging disorder

As with a number of other matters relating to hypnosis there is no proof that an existing disorder in a person can be prolonged when a hypnotic trance is induced. However, West and Deckert (1965, p. 97) inform us there is indirect and inferential evidence that disorders require continuing alternative treatment to hypnotherapy, beyond the time when the disorder would normally have considerably improved, or even been cured.

Risk of superficial relief

Relief from symptoms may be achieved upon a person being treated by hypnosis for a particular complaint. However, sometimes only the symptom and not the root cause of the physical illness or mental disorder that is alleviated.

For example, a subject being treated for persistent attacks of migraine – for which hypnotherapy is particularly well suited and invariably successful – could obtain relief from the pain, but unbeknown to both the client and hypnotherapist, the pain was emanating from a tumour on the brain. Thus, whilst superficial relief can be achieved, an underlying ailment can progress undetected, because the symptom has been removed.

Here again it is debatable whether injury has been *caused* by the hypnosis but the point is arguable, in a similar manner to making an existing disorder worse.

Categories of the Risks of Hypnosis

The methodology adopted in writing about the risks of hypnosis to classify them according to one of five different categories and then evaluate them. By this means all of the cases reviewed are collected together in separate chapters according to category. Naturally, a few studies qualify for more than one category.

Six surveys

These six clinical, experimental and stage hypnosis studies involve various methods of data collection connected with the risks of hypnosis and associated adverse psychological effects. These different methods of data collection make meta-analytical of the studies impossible, but they collectively form a most useful basis of reference regarding each of the risks of hypnosis.

Hypnosis per se *and therapeutic use*

These categories demonstrate how serious adverse effects are more likely to arise from hypnosis in therapeutic use than the application of hypnosis alone. Furthermore, it emphasises the importance of properly trained persons using hypnosis for therapeutic use. This does not mean that their clients do not experience adverse effects, far from it but, they are better equipped to deal with such effects.

Failure to terminate

A number of case studies relate the consequences of a hypnotic trance not being terminated, which can produce serious after effects. This category, of the risks of hypnosis, offers clinical evidence that a proper termination of a trance is vital.

Coercion

Even though coercion under hypnosis, or by posthypnotic suggestion, is not an after effect which alone is deleterious to the subject's health, it can still be dangerous and is therefore included as a category.

On stage

Unlike the therapeutic use of hypnosis, and contrary to popular belief, this category reveals that there may only be one danger arising directly from the hypnotic procedure. On stage hypnosis is often mentioned in this book and is the setting for what appears to be the only reported legal case.

It would be unfair to allow the nature of hypnosis to shoulder all the blame for all adverse effects. Therefore, some of the effects that can be generated by the hypnotiser are also highlighted.

Chapter 5

Six Case Studies

Josephine R. Hilgard (1974)
'Sequelae to Hypnosis'

The surveys contained in this journal article was written by Hilgard, a psychiatrist of the Department of Psychology at Stanford University, California, and part of the University's Hypnosis Research Program.

It should be explained that the strict meaning of the word 'sequelae', used by Hilgard in the title to her study, is morbid affections following a disease. However, Hilgard restricts the morbid or sickly affections to hypnosis. The objective of Hilgard's study was to gather evidence of the possible after effects of hypnosis – which she admits may be produced in some people – because practising hypnotists need to be aware of these possibilities.

Hilgard is quick to point out that there is a difference between laboratory hypnosis, which is the setting for her study, and clinical hypnosis. The former is episodic and impersonal, whilst the latter is of an enduring, therapeutic and personal nature. Surprisingly, most reports of problems caused by hypnosis come from therapeutic use. Hilgard cites Levitt and Hershman (1963) who found that one in four members of a (therapeutic) hypnosis society, who completed questionnaires, had observed unusual reactions (adverse effects) to hypnosis.

The subjects of Hilgard's study were university students drawn from '[…] A normal university population […]' which thereby '[…] Minimized the therapeutic interactions.' (p. 282). This means that each of the subjects was deemed unlikely to have a pre-existing condition. This, combined with the hypnosis being induced in a laboratory setting, theoretically restricts any after effects to hypnosis alone, rather than hypnosis mixed with the application of therapies.

It is important to consider whether a particular after effect, no matter how it arises, comprises an 'injury' within the meaning of an illegal assault. This is something to be crucially considered in all the studies.

After hypnosis each of the one hundred and twenty students was individually interviewed with particular reference to any after effects they had experienced. They were questioned about specific after effects, which Hilgard had noted over the years, such as, drowsiness, headaches and confusion. Hilgard was careful to obtain an estimate of the endurance of the after effects, particularly those that had gone within an hour (called 'short-term effects') and those which lasted more than an hour ('long-term effects').

At this stage the reader should be reminded that in the previous chapter, when discussing psychological injury, it was stated that such injury did not qualify as an 'injury' within the meaning of assault if it was of a temporary or minor nature. It was also stated that DSM-IV could form a reasonable benchmark to adopt in determining what constitutes a qualifying psychological injury. It is, therefore, a matter of applying these principles to the nature of the after effects recorded by Hilgard. Naturally, the same principles apply to other authors' findings in the following five surveys and elsewhere in this dissertation. It can then be decided if hypnosis has caused any psychological injury or harm to any of the subjects, which could properly form part of an illegal assault.

First of all, Hilgard tabulates short- and long-term somatic (pertaining to the body, but more than likely linked to psychological factors) effects in the short-term as 1 student developed a headache and 1 a stiff neck. Long-term effects were 3 students with headaches, 1 with dizziness and nausea, 1 with a stiff arm and 1 with a stiff neck.

Hilgard does not provide any information with regard to the method of induction she used. If the 'Eye Fixation with Progressive Relaxation' technique was employed (part of the Permissive Method) a stiff neck could result. A stiff arm could result from using Erickson's hand levitation technique (part of the Intermediate Method) (see Chapter 2). It could be argued that the stiff necks and arms were not after effects directly arising from the hypnotic trance itself.

In any event, these somatic after effects, being of a temporary nature and of a common everyday nature, are not acceptable as injuries within the meaning of assault even though somatoform disorder is listed in DSM-IV. The somatoform disorder listed in DSM-IV (See Part I of Appendix B (p. 191)) refers to recurrent and multiple physical symptoms for which there are no apparent physical causes. These are clearly not the somatic after effects Hilgard alludes to.

The psychological after effects in Hilgard's study were reported as: 8 students short-term and 7 long-term from drowsiness and sleep, 8 short-term and 2 long-term from cognitive distortion and confusion, 1 short-term from anxiety and 4 long-term from night dreams (Table 2, p. 287).

Excluding somatic symptoms, the long and short-term after effects together affected twenty-five percent of the 120 students, but only one is mentioned in DSM-IV – anxiety. It was for less than one hour and of a very temporary nature and therefore this particular after effect would not form part of an illegal assault.

The long-term effects of the two students suffering from cognitive distortion and confusion are not included in DSM-IV, because whilst they may be symptoms of a disorder they do not constitute a disorder by themselves, either singularly or jointly. Confusion is included MacHovec's list of complications (see Part II of Appendix B (p. 193)). The reference to cognitive distortion is not to be interpreted as depersonalisation disorder (see DSM-IV list under main heading of 'Dissociative disorders' in Part I of Appendix B (p. 191)) where one's body feels altered in size and perceived from a distance. These two cases of cognitive distortion and confusion were both of a minor nature and, in any event, if they had been chronic in MacHovec's terms (i.e. months or years), Hilgard would most definitely have said so.

To summarise, there were no after effects in any of the one hundred and twenty students, which qualified as psychological injury within the meaning of an illegal assault. However, Hilgard's study was restricted to after effects caused by hypnosis alone and involved subjects who were considered unlikely to suffer from any pre-existing psychological condition.

'Attitudes of Psychiatrists to the Use of Hypnosis' Alfred Auerback (1962)

This journal article was written by Auerback whilst he was a Professor of Psychiatry at the University of California School of Medicine and presented to a meeting of the American Psychiatric Association.

The main objective of a questionnaire sent out by Auerback was to ascertain the extent of the use of hypnosis by psychiatrists in California. The questionnaire was sent to 828 psychiatrists of which 414 replied and of that number 192 were experienced with hypnotisers. Included in the questionnaire were questions about 'untoward results associated with hypnosis'.

Auerback lists the 201 untoward results reported, with which the psychiatrists '[...] Were personally acquainted' (p. 919). Even though the questionnaires were only sent to psychiatrists, the returns included untoward results from other hypnotists that the psychiatrists were personally acquainted – with a reference to patients who subsequently came under the care of the respondent psychiatrists after suffering untoward results during, or after hypnosis induced by others.

By far the largest category was 'psychosis precipitated' at 113 cases out of the grand total of 201. Remember, a disorder may not be complete and apparent, but can be triggered, or precipitated, by hypnosis and thereafter take full effect. The reports do not suggest that the induction of a hypnotic trance, or subsequent procedures, caused a disorder. While psychoses are most certainly well represented within DSM-IV and are likely to be of a chronic nature, their pre-existing condition means that the 113 cases of psychoses precipitated do not qualify as an injury forming part of an illegal assault.

The 23 cases of untoward results next listed by Auerback and labelled 'symptoms unchanged, recurred, or replaced' are also presaged by existing conditions, and thereby do not count as injuries comprising an illegal assault.

Auerback then lists 'panic or extreme anxiety' (23 cases) as an untoward result. Here, there are two alternative conditions stated, both anxiety based. Reber (1995), in *Dictionary of Psychology*, defines 'anxiety' and 'panic attack' as follows:

Anxiety

[…] A vague, unpleasant emotional state with qualities of apprehension, dread, distress and uneasiness. (P. 45.)

Panic attack

A discrete period of intense fear or discomfort accompanied by various symptoms which may include shortness of breath, dizziness, palpitations, trembling, sweating, nausea and often a fear that one is going crazy. The attacks […] typically last no longer than 15 minutes. (P. 533.)

Panic attack appears under the main heading of 'Anxiety' in DSM-IV (See Part I of Appendix B (p. 199)) and, therefore, it appears that psychological injury *has* arisen in a form which satisfies the criteria of illegal assault. Anxiety and panic attacks may be of a transient nature, thereby disallowing the injury as a part of such illegal assault, but Auerback continues: 'The occurrence of acute anxiety, panic states, […] following hypnosis had resulted in patients seeking psychiatric help.' (p. 920). There can be no doubt that these untoward results of 'panic or extreme anxiety' were not of a transient nature – in the sense that they were recurring – and therefore, they count as injuries within the meaning of illegal assault.

'Excessive dependency' is another of Auerback's untoward results (8 cases). This arises, within the context of his study, when patients became excessively reliant upon the hypnotising psychiatrist for emotional support. This is not a disorder listed in DSM-IV and therefore not the type of injury in which this book is concerned.

Listed by Auerback is 'depression, suicide' (6 cases). This is obviously not depression which everyone feels from time to time and which Reber (1995, p. 533) describes as:

> Generally, a mood state characterized by a sense of inadequacy, a feeling of despondency, a decrease in activity or reactivity, pessimism, sadness and related symptoms. In this sense depressions are quite normal, relatively shortlived and (damnably) frequent.

Depression is listed as being conjoined with suicide as an untoward result and it is, therefore, safe to assume that it is neither of a temporary nature, nor a common everyday occurrence.

At the time Auerback wrote his article there were two principal forms of clinical depression – now contained under the heading of 'Mood disorder' in DSM-IV – known as endogenous and reactive. Both forms of depression were classified as neuroses, as opposed to the more serious and severe psychoses, described in Chapter Five. Endogenous depression results from internal factors with no apparent precipitating event. Reactive depression results from events occurring in one's everyday life. It is likely that the depression caused by hypnosis is of the reactive type.

These cases of depression constitute a psychological injury within the terms of our meaning of illegal assault.

Auerback's list continues with 3 cases of 'acting out', which are uninhibited displays of feelings and emotions, and are not included in DSM-IV. In any event, emotion does not properly form part of an assault.

'Sexual seduction' (3 cases) is not, of course, within DSM-IV.

There are 3 cases of 'conversion symptoms' on Auerback's list of untoward results. Conversion is the transformation of a psychological maladjustment into a physical form, which, in these three cases, strongly suggest pre-existing adverse psychological disorders. These situations are pre-existing conditions, as is 'masked organic disease' (1 case), which is the last untoward result on Auerback's list. In both, there is no injury that could form part of illegal assault.

To summarise one can state, that out of 201 untoward results in Auerback's study, twenty six cases of 'panic or extreme anxiety' and 6 cases of 'depression, suicide' appear to qualify as injury, within the meaning of illegal assault.

'Clinicians' perceptions of the adverse effects of hypnosis' Judd, Burrows and Dennerstein (1986)

Fiona K. Judd, Graham D. Burrows and Lorraine Dennerstein were staff researchers of Melbourne University, Australia and also of a hospital psychiatric department when they wrote the above journal article, which was based upon a questionnaire constructed from responses from twenty members of the Executive of the International Society of Hypnosis.

The primary objective of the questionnaire was to solicit practitioners' perceptions of possible adverse effects of hypnosis when used therapeutically. It was sent to all members of the Australian Society of Hypnosis, and 202 members responded, all of whom used hypnosis. This sample comprised 133 medical practitioners, 16 dentists and 53 psychologists. Eighty-eight respondents (43.5%) reported that some patients had experienced adverse effects. Fourteen types of adverse effects were reported.

Judd *et al* tabulated a number of types of adverse effects only in general terms: Fantasised Sexual Seduction (8 cases), Difficulty Terminating Trance (25 cases), During Treatment of Children (4 cases), Problems Encountered in Management of Childbirth (3 cases) and Patient Coerced to Acts Without Consent (1 case). Apart from difficulty terminating the trance, very little, or no detail at all is supplied concerning these types of adverse effects. Therefore, because of their lack of real detail, it is reasonable to assume that no psychological injury or harm emanated from them.

The reports of difficulty terminating the trance relates to a patient who remained in a semi-dissociated state for several hours and a patient who was disorientated, confused and unable to keep awake. Apart from being of a minor nature these symptoms were transient, and not being contained in DSM-IV, so cannot be regarded as injuries.

There are other types of adverse effects listed by Judd *et al* that can be grouped together as pre-existing conditions (see subheading of 'After effects not coincident with use of hypnosis' in Chapter 4).

The first of this group of adverse effects is Symptom Substitution (reported by 16 practitioners), which as a pre-existing condition is regarded as 'Making an existing disorder worse'. The second adverse effect is Worsening Psychosis (5 practitioners), again a pre-existing condition, being in the category 'Making an existing condition worse'. The third adverse effect of Precipitating Psychosis' (5 practitioners) fits very neatly into the pre-existing condition of the 'Danger of precipitating a mental disorder'. The fourth and final adverse effect of this group is Injudicious Symptom Removal in Presence of Organic Disease (3 practitioners). This adverse effect is most certainly another pre-existing condition of the kind where there is a 'Danger of superficial relief' only. Judd *et al* illustrate this case, with an example of a patient who was hypnotically treated for the alleviation of pain in the right iliac fossa (hollow in the inner side of the pelvis). This patient required emergency surgery twelve hours later for an acute appendicitis, even though still not in pain.

Two types of listed adverse effects, Excessive Dependency (patient becomes excessively reliant upon practitioner for emotional support) (25 practitioners) and Acting Out Behaviour (uninhibited displays of feelings and emotions) (9 practitioners) are patently not relevant in this study of injury as part of illegal assault.

Judd *et al* also recorded reports of Suicidal Behaviour in Depressed patients (3 practitioners). The wording of this adverse effect is properly interpreted as suicidal behaviour developing in patients, who were already suffering from one of the depressive disorders which are listed in DSM-IV. In this case the depression has not been caused by the hypnosis and, as a result, does not qualify as an injury.

The final type of adverse effect is Development of Panic/Extreme Anxiety. Fifty-three practitioners, out of the 88 who responded to the questionnaire, had experience of this effect in their patients. Judd *et al* write:

> The most frequently reported adverse effect was the development of extreme anxiety and panic. The responses (from the practitioners) do not allow us to establish the cause or duration of such anxiety in many cases. Anxiety or panic is usually immediately evident and readily recognized and thus most likely to be reported. (p. 57)

It seems that the authors could neither be certain of the duration of some of the adverse effects, nor the cause. This uncertainty makes it impossible to be sure if any of the adverse effects of the nature of Development of Panic/Extreme Anxiety constitute injury as part of an illegal assault. Clearly, some of these latter adverse effects could be injuries forming part of illegal assault, but there is, of course, no conclusive evidence.

'The Clinical Practice of Hypnosis in the United States' Eugene E. Levitt and Seymour Hershman (1962)

Levitt was a medical doctor and clinical psychologist of the Indiana University Medical Centre when this article was written. The study is based on the results of a questionnaire sent to members of the American Society of Clinical Hypnosis and the Society for Clinical and Experimental Hypnosis.

One of the objectives of the survey was to record unusual reactions to being hypnotised experienced by clinical practitioners in their patients. The practitioner respondents were mainly medical doctors (70%), with some specialising in obstetrics, gynaecology, psychiatry, surgery and anaesthesiology. The other respondents were dentists. Only five psychologists were included in the sample, out of a total of 21 individuals involved in the mental health professions.

An analysis of 298 returns revealed 83 practitioners had noted an unusual reaction to hypnosis. Levitt *et al* tabulate only when at least three respondents reported the same reaction. This aspect of the design was included to ensure the genuineness of each of the listed unusual reactions.

Levitt *et al* generally define unusual reactions as, '[…] An unusual, unexpected, and probably alarming, reaction to hypnosis, either during the state itself, or immediately afterwards.' (p. 59).

Many of the unusual reactions listed by Levitt *et al* are not sufficient for this guide, because they are either clearly of a temporary nature, emotional (see Chapter 4), of a minor nature, or do not appear in DSM-IV. In any one of these circumstances the unusual results would not amount to injury. Such discounted results are: Headache, vomiting, fainting, dizziness etc. (15 cases); Crying and hysteria (9 cases); Loss of rapport during hypnosis (7 cases); Difficulties involving sex (5 cases); Excessive dependency on hypnotist (3 cases); and Difficulty resulting from inadvertently given suggestions (3 cases).

Five cases of 'Overt psychosis after hypnosis' were reported, indicates precipitating a psychosis as a pre-existing condition and thereby they do not qualify as an injury.

Finally, Levitt *et al* list 'Emotional upset, anxiety or panic, or depression' (29 cases) as unusual reactions. Even though these reactions are joined together as a group, each is a distinct and separate unusual reactions.

The first of these unusual reactions is 'emotional upset' which can be eliminated as an injury for the purpose of establishing an illegal assault, because it is minor in nature and emotional in content.

The second unusual reaction of this group is 'anxiety or panic attack' which, at face value, qualify as injuries, as part of an illegal assault. However, there is no information to suggest that the anxiety or panic attacks were a single short-lived episode, or of a chronic nature. The former could be classified as transient and disqualified as constituting injury as part of an illegal assault, but not so the latter event.

The third unusual reaction of the group is 'depression'. This could refer to ordinary everyday depression, or to clinical depression. It is reasonable to assume that if Levitt *et al* list other everyday occurrences, such as headache and nausea, that commonplace depression would be treated in like manner. However, it would also be a reasonable assumption that depression of the type contained in DSM-IV forms part of Levitt *et al*'s 'depression' and thereby constitutes injury for the purpose of illegal assault, but there is no clue in Levitt *et al*'s journal article indicating to what sort of depression they are referring. A question mark must hang over this unusual reaction of depression and in these circumstances it must be discounted as an injury to form part of illegal assault.

None of the reactions mentioned by Levitt *et al* can be said, with any degree of certainty, to form part of an illegal assault. It is likely that some of the unusual reactions are likely to be injuries forming part of illegal assault. But there is no proof of this.

'Hypnosis and Risks to Human Subjects' William C. Coe and Klazina Ryken (1979)

Coe, a psychologist, was a member of the teaching staff at California State University and Ryken, his pupil, was a master's degree student when this paper was written. The subjects were psychology students at the same university.

The study was concerned with the degree of risk associated with hypnosis and involved comparing the after effects of hypnosis upon seventy students with the after effects of: Participating in a brief verbal learning experience (35 students); Taking a college exam (35 students); Attending a college class (35 students); and College life in general (35 students).

The negative sequelae listed by Coe and Ryken are; headache, upset stomach, stiff neck, light headed, dizzy, vague, anxious, fearful, depressed and unhappy. Only two of these after effects – anxious and depressed – might qualify as injury within the meaning of illegal assault, because the others are clearly of a minor nature and largely ordinary, everyday. Coe and Ryken imply the transient and minor nature of all the after effects when they write:

> [...] Since all subjects were informed that they were free to contact us further about any difficulties they wished to discuss (a standard safeguard we always employ) and none of our subjects chose to contact us, we have indirect evidence that the sequelae were not that troublesome. (P. 679.)

The authors conclude that, 'The results indicate that hypnosis is no more bothersome than are the comparison activities.' (p. 673).

In Coe and Ryken's study it can be confidently stated that no injury exists of the nature required to complete an illegal assault.

'Impact of Stage Hypnosis,' Lennis G. Echterling and David A. Emmerling (1987)

This article was based on a paper presented at the 1984 American Psychological Association Annual meeting when both the authors were university faculty members. The purpose of the study was to assess the impact of a performance by a stage hypnotist upon university students, of which some were in the audience and others in a trance upon the stage. This book is, for the moment, only interested in the negative experiences of both groups during, and after being in a hypnotic trance. A comparison of the adverse after effects, particularly of a serious nature, generated by stage hypnotists as opposed to other hypnotists, is a matter for consideration later (see Chapter 9).

Echterling and Emmerling carried out two surveys, one by telephone and the other by face-to-face interviews. The telephone survey was made up of 292 students who were in the audience. Surprisingly, it revealed that 32% of this group described the experience in a negative manner, using such terms as 'weird' and 'exploitive'. Only two of these respondents reported adverse after effects of 'feeling apprehensive' and 'frightened' and also being controlled by the hypnotist. None of these negative experiences and after effects amounts to injury to satisfy illegal assault.

Eighteen students, who had been on the stage in a trance, were questioned in greater depth in face-to-face interviews. Some of the reported negative experiences are interesting and worth repeating, even though they do not amount to psychological injury. Four of these students complained in negative terms. One said, "I didn't want to do what the hypnotist said [...] I felt embarrassed and scared." Another, "I knew what I was doing, but I had no control [...]. It bothered me [...] I was scared I might fall when I was running." The third student was frightened she might be selected for past life regression. The final subject thought her experience was very traumatic, "I didn't want to go into a trance [...] I tried to wake up, but I couldn't [...] When I finally did come out of the trance, I was terrified [...] I ran out of the auditorium, down the hall, and started to cross the field when a security guard caught me [and] brought me back [...] I thought the hypnotist was really evil.

[He suggested that I] come back in and watch the show. I was still scared and hated him, but I had to go back in." (pp. 151–2).

Echterling and Emmerling report that five of the other on stage students had negative after effects. One stated that she was now afraid of hypnosis and felt embarrassed by her performance. Another said she was, 'spaced out occasionally' and felt others perceived her as more moody and quiet. The next subject related how some days after the stage event she entered a trance upon hearing harmonica music on the radio. The fourth subject described how she behaved in a manic fashion for about six hours after the show and was unable to sleep.

The last of the five students' accounts of negative after effects were more serious and dramatic. The student stated, "I didn't sleep for the next two days. I hibernated and hid from everybody. It has still left me shook up. I'm going to drop out of school […]. This has messed up everything. I lost control […]. This forces me to think about stuff I don't want to." (p. 152). From this brief dialogue it is, of course, impossible for anyone to diagnose what particular psychological disorder, if any, from which this student was suffering. Furthermore, it is not known how long the after effects lasted or whether the student did 'drop out' of college. However, in the event of the undoubted adverse psychological condition continuing for some time and it being of the nature of Anxiety (seemingly without panic attacks) and/or Mood disorder (depression) specified in DSM-IV, one could label this condition as a psychological injury which suits an illegal assault.

We can speculate that perhaps only one qualifying illegal assault injury was caused by the on stage hypnosis (i.e. the Anxiety and/or Mood Disorder), and perhaps in this case there was a pre-existing condition, of which we have no knowledge.

Chapter 6

Dangers of Hypnosis – **per se** *and Therapeutic Use*

The induction of a hypnotic trance can take place in laboratory, clinical and non-clinical settings. This chapter distinguishes between laboratory and clinical contexts to assess the dangers associated with therapeutic use. The non-clinical setting is covered in Chapter 9.

The basic difference between laboratory and clinical setting is the use in the laboratory, for research and experimental purposes is theoretically that of hypnosis only, whereas clinical use is based upon the application of therapies. Hypnosis is not, of course, a treatment, but it is the means by which treatment may be applied.

The induction of a trance in the laboratory context is regarded as episodic in the sense that it is a relatively well defined occurrence, regarded as a complete event. However, in the therapeutic setting it is expected that by combining the application of therapies with hypnosis, changes will take place in the behaviour and personality of the subject.

Hypnosis in a Laboratory Setting

In Chapter 5, Hilgard's study was based on research in a laboratory, with university students as the subjects. It was designed to record the after effects of hypnosis *per se* (the application of hypnosis only) upon them. Hilgard thought that subjects drawn from a university population were unlikely to suffer from any pre-existing conditions (see Chapter 5).

In 1965, Martin T. Orne, an American university and hospital psychiatrist, published the results of a study similar to Hilgard's (1974). Selected students were hypnotised in a laboratory setting without, of course, therapies being involved. All of the several thousand college students hypnotised, were informed of the 'experimental', rather than the 'therapeutic', nature of the research and also that no treatment was involved. Furthermore, any student hoping for self-improvement or requesting help (e.g. with examination nerves, stopping smoking or nail biting) was excluded as were those with obvious mental disorder. Orne confidently writes

> Thus the situation is defined explicitly as episodic, therefore assurances are given that, at the completion of the experiment, the individual will be exactly as he was when he began. No permanent change, either positive or negative, may legitimately be expected. (1965, p. 227.)

The nature of the adverse effects recorded by both Orne and Hilgard were identical in that they consisted, amongst other things, of headaches, drowsiness, and nausea. In addition, all the effects were transient. In other words the adverse effects in both studies were most certainly of a minor and temporary nature and do not constitute injury for the purpose of an illegal assault.

At first, it seems in the Orne (1965) study, the low incidence of minor adverse effects could be partly ascribed to screening students; students with an obvious pre-existing condition were eliminated. However, this is not the case. Later in his article Orne informs us that the screening is extremely superficial and that '[...] Student volunteers include a goodly percentage of individuals with considerable psychopathology, [...].' In addition, there is no mention of screening when Orne summarises the relationship of hypnosis and adverse effects, in a laboratory setting, as follows:

> [...] It seems that the induction of hypnosis itself does not lead to untoward consequences if it is perceived as relatively *episodic nonpersonal* viz. if the subject does not expect to be changed in any way and does not perceive the procedure as directed personally at him.

This means in both the Orne and Hilgard studies the presence of pre-existing conditions was not a factor which was affected by hypnosis *per se.*

In Faw, Sellers and Wilcox's experimental study of negative effects arising in college student subjects the '[...] more maladjusted persons of the population sample' were deliberately included in the trials. It was concluded '[...] That there are nondetrimental effects when hypnosis is used with a normal college population'. This conclusion must not be interpreted as meaning that there were no detrimental effects because the subjects were drawn from a normal college population, but merely means that the trials were restricted to students. The fact that this and other studies cited involve college students does not mean that the concept of the use of hypnosis in the laboratory, without serious adverse effects, is inappropriate to subjects who are not college students. The experimenters used students because they were at the same university and willing to volunteer in return for payment, or a psychology course credit. It is clear from these studies that hypnosis is unlikely to cause or precipitate adverse effects of a nature which amount to anything other than minor and transient adverse effects, provided it is an episodic event administered in laboratory conditions.

However, Orne would have one believe initially that those subjects with 'obvious psychopathology' should be excluded from participating in researches. While the emphasis is upon *obvious* psychopathology this exclusion is not necessary to preclude the more serious adverse effects arising, in addition to minor and transient effects. First, Orne's disclosure that the student subjects included those with 'considerable psychopathology'. Second, the Faw *et al* study included so-called 'maladjusted persons' and yet only minor and transient adverse effects were reported. Finally, Hilgard took no measures to eliminate any subjects with psychological disorders and again only minor and transient untoward effects were recorded. It seems that the view concerning the exclusion of those subjects with psychopathologies ('pre-existing conditions'), in the laboratory context, has changed to the extent that no importance is placed on it any longer.

In a 1982 experimental study, Helen J. Crawford, Josephine R. Hilgard and Hugh MacDonald, all of the prestigious American Stanford University, investigated transient experiences following hypnosis. The experiment was designed to compare the anticipated transient effects after hypnosis in a laboratory setting between group induced hypnosis and individuals alone.

Crawford *et al* reported:

> Similar to percentages before, in the present study 5% of Ss reported transient experiences of a negative nature following the group HGSHS:A, while 29% of Ss reported them following the individual SHSS:C.

> HGSHS:A (Harvard Group Scale of Hypnotic Susceptibility: Form A, of Shor and Orne (1962)) and SHSS:C (Stanford Hypnotic Susceptibility Scale: Form C, of Weitzenhoffer and Hilgard (1959)) are standardised forms of the application of hypnosis. The former is designed for group hypnosis and is ideomotor orientated (e.g. hand movements and arm rigidity) and the latter is for individuals and is cognitively based (e.g. carrying out a mental task during induction).

In those studies requiring a large number of subjects to be hypnotised, it would be impossible without being able to induce a trance in a group of subjects simultaneously. This method of hypnotism also ensures that exactly the same wording – taken from HGSHS – is used for all subjects.

The Crawford *et al* study reported minor and transient negative after effects of drowsiness, headaches, nausea, dreams and cognitive disorientation, among the 172 students who were hypnotised during the course of the experiment.

The experimental evidence suggests that hypnosis in a laboratory setting is likely to be associated with minor and transient adverse effects only, the combination of hypnosis with therapy must be investigated as a possible source of danger to the subject.

Hypnosis in a Clinical Setting

Surprisingly, more serious hypnotic adverse effects occur in the therapeutic context, where ameliorative reaction is expected when a trance is induced for the purpose of the application of therapies. It is even more surprising when considering the relatively high number of serious effects reported by experienced therapists, who are often medically qualified (see Auerback (1962), to the relatively small number of minor and transient reactions in the laboratory setting.

Karle (1991, p. 187) provides a logical explanation for this apparent anomaly when he proposes:

> [...] hypnotic techniques can have significant effects on all physical aspects
> of human functioning, from the arteries to viscera, and equally, on psychic
> processes. If hypnosis can affect these functions therapeutically, then it can
> do so pathogenically. And if that is the case, it is potentially dangerous.

It is a relatively simple matter to compare the adverse effects arising between the two situations.

In the two laboratory based studies, the adverse effects were of
both a minor and transient nature, but that was not the case with
the studies which were therapeutically related, when serious
adverse effects were recorded. The most frequent of the more serious effects were anxiety (with and without panic attacks) and
depression, which in Auerback's study led to some cases of suicide. Both these effects are listed in DSM-IV (see Chapter 4 and
Part I of Appendix B (p. 191)) and qualify as injury as part of illegal assault. Here one can see the difference in practice between
minor and temporary adverse effects, by way of ordinary everyday
complaints (e.g. headaches, dizziness and nausea), arising in a laboratory setting and the more serious adverse effects in a clinical
context.

Orne and other writers explain this danger of hypnosis in therapeutic use on the basis that they are not episodic. In therapeutic use
the therapist aims to make a relatively permanent change in the
subject's symptoms. These symptoms serve some purpose within
the unconscious mind, and can be difficult to abandon. It logically
follows that unconsciously the subject is ambivalent about the
treatment achieving its objective. Thus, the induction of a hypnotic
trance can easily be perceived by the subject as a threat to that part
of the unconscious mind which was adjusted in the first instance
and produce the unwanted symptoms. Therefore, it is the perceived threat, that is likely to be responsible for precipitating
adverse effects. This threat is not present in an episodic event in a
laboratory setting.

In addition to endorsing that hypnosis *per se* is unlikely to produce
after effects other than of a minor and transient nature, Crawford
et al (1982) was another interesting aspect relevant to the dangers
of the therapeutic use of hypnosis. Of the reported fourteen cases
of cognitive disorientation only one occurred when employing
HGSHS:A. The remainder occurred using the cognitively based

SHSS:C. So the higher percentage of the overall adverse effects were attributable to SHSS:C. It would be logical to think, that if any serious adverse effects were to be precipitated by the induction of a hypnotic trance, it would be one that was cognitively based, particularly in view of the large number of cognitively based mental disorders contained in DSM-IV. Giving up smoking is a good example of serious after effects being generated by the threat, or perceived threat, of the application of therapy, not by hypnosis *per se*.

A person becomes addicted to smoking tobacco for one of two reasons. Either, because it is a habit and is, for example, acquired as a youth, having a wish to appear 'grown up' and be 'one of the boys'. Or, as a result of a traumatic event, such as the unexpected death of a close family member, whereupon comfort is sought from smoking cigarettes.

There are very different therapeutic scripts to be applied when treating each of these two situations and the reader may wonder how the therapist knows which one to apply. The method employed is first of all to induce a trance and then ask the client, or more accurately to ask the client's unconscious mind, the reason he or she first started to smoke. An ideomotor response is used, such as raising a finger on one hand to indicate 'no' and on the other hand 'yes'.

In respect of 'habit' smoking it may be that the habit becomes part of an existing personality trait which, according to Eysenck, is relatively enduring and difficult to change. In these circumstances the unconscious mind considers the induction of a hypnotic trance, for the purpose of a proposed personality change, as a threat. By this means injury may arise from the use of this particular therapy.

In the case of the 'traumatic event' smoker there is a much simpler explanation of why, for example, anxiety attacks can arise upon the proposed application of therapy under hypnosis. In this case the threat is to the 'comfort' obtained from smoking, which if removed may awaken the unwanted negative feelings surrounding the original traumatic event which started the subject smoking.

Even in the more specialised branches of the medical profession, where hypnosis is used for therapeutic purposes, the view is the same as Orne and other writers on the topic of the dangers of hypnosis in a clinical setting. For example, Doctor Jacob H. Conn writes:

> There are no significant or specific dangers associated with hypnosis *per se*. The actual dangers are those which accompany every psychotherapeutic relationship. (1972, p. 61.)

In another branch of the medical profession, that of dentistry, we are informed (Kleinhauz *et al* (1987)) that complications rarely arise from hypnosis, because the induction of a trance is regarded as an episodic event, used only for the purpose of easing discomfort and relaxation. In this circumstance the patient regards the hypnosis as nothing more than a technique to assist the dental treatment with analgesia and relaxation. As a result it is certainly not perceived as being utilised in conjunction with therapies, where an alteration to the patient's psyche (the mind in this context) is sought.

Both the episodic nature and the emphasis on non-therapeutic use in a dental surgery – regarded as being in a laboratory context – is provided by Doctor Moris Kleinhauz and Ilana Eli, both of Tel Aviv University Dental School, in a 1987 journal article.

One of the four case studies in the article concerns a female patient who easily achieved a deep trance so that complete anaesthesia was possible to allow treatment. The patient was so impressed by the possibilities of hypnosis she begged the dental surgeon to stop her smoking. He agreed, and applied the therapy at a subsequent session. At this point the episodic nature of hypnosis ceased and became therapeutic. The patient stopped smoking, but a short time thereafter she developed an anxiety/depressive reaction with obsessive thoughts of whether or not to start smoking again. In addition she became unable to cope with everyday activities, was hospitalised and diagnosed with decompensation (failure of resistance to complaints which leads to exacerbation of one's condition) of an obsessive neurosis. She was cured first of her mental disorder by referral to her dentist who allowed her to smoke again, but still required further psychiatric treatment for her underlying psychological condition.

There appears to be no doubt that the mere transfer, from what is regarded as an episodic to a nonepisodic setting, created the very serious mental disorder in the patient. This case study of Kleinhauz and Eli is an excellent example of the dangers of hypnosis in a clinical setting, as opposed to the use for research and experimentation in a laboratory setting.

According to Kleinhauz (1987, p. 158):

> The use by dentists to induce anaesthesia and relaxation generally places only minimal hazards. The practitioner's goals in such settings are specific and limited to his area of professional competence [...]. Any attempt to depart from the context of his profession may lead to severe problems.

It is clear from studies such as Orne, Faw *et al* and Hilgard that hypnosis *per se* is most unlikely to have any affect upon the so-called pre-existing conditions. Furthermore, it is equally as clear that the dangers associated with pre-existing conditions can be realised when therapy under hypnosis is applied.

Proving a link between pre-existing conditions and adverse effects upon the induction of a hypnotic trance is important to a researcher. If this link is neither established nor eliminated, it would be most difficult, if not in some cases impossible, to separate hypnosis *per se* and hypnosis with therapy, as precipitators of serious adverse effects. Research suggests that pre-existing conditions are apparently not linked to serious adverse effects. **So, hypnosis *per se* can be eliminated as being associated with the production of the previously defined injury as part of an illegal assault, but not when it is coupled with therapy.**

Orne (1965, p. 236) concludes the discussion on the dangers of hypnosis in therapeutic use:

> [...] In some situations seem to occur very rarely. These include the setting of the research laboratory, and the analgesic use of hypnosis in medicine and dentistry. It is characteristic of these situations that the subject's encounter with hypnosis is episodic. [...] The chances of trouble are much greater when the hypnosis is used therapeutically, and indeed it is the therapeutic context which has produced most of the reported difficulties. The mere induction of hypnosis by a therapist can be threatening to the patient's system of defenses, and may result in an anxiety attack.

Chapter 7

Dangers of Hypnosis – Failure to Terminate

There are three circumstances where failure of trance termination (also called 'dehypnotisation') can arise: (1) The inadequate termination procedures adopted by the hypnotiser; (2) Where no attempt whatsoever is made to terminate; and (3) Where the subject has no wish to return to the fully conscious waking state and prefers to remain in a hypnotic trance. There are significant differences between the failure by a hypnotist to dehypnotise and failure of a trance to terminate for another reason, but both are dangers of hypnosis.

It has already been explained in Chapter 2 that it is most important to properly and thoroughly terminate a hypnotic trance (see Appendix A, Part V (p. 187) for termination script) otherwise danger can arise.

The failure of a hypnotic trance to terminate, for whatever reason, can occur in all three major settings, that is, in the laboratory, clinic, and on stage, as well as involving amateurs (usually comprising students experimenting with hypnosis for fun).

It could be argued that any adverse effects, arising from the refusal of a subject to return to the full waking state, are self-inflicted and as a result outside the scope of this good practice guide. However, for the purpose of this guide, it is assumed that any of these adverse effects arise directly from the hypnotic trance, or the behaviour of the hypnotiser, and as a consequence can be considered as properly forming part of an illegal assault.

This chapter examines the three reasons for a trance not terminating and illustrates them with case studies. The main purpose of this examination is to determine if any serious adverse effects arising from nontermination can be regarded as injury, listed in DSM-IV, and thereby forming part of an illegal assault.

Hypnotist's failure to terminate

Laboratory setting

There are no reported cases of a hypnotiser in a laboratory setting failing to properly and thoroughly terminating a trance, or making no attempt to terminate, resulting in serious adverse psychological effects. There are some cases of a subject refusing to be dehypnotised, such as Sakata (1968) which is referred to later in this chapter.

Initially, it seemed that this situation was connected with there being no serious adverse effects arising in the laboratory setting from hypnosis *per se* (see Chapter 6). However, this cannot be the case because the induction of a trance is often accompanied by other hypnotic procedures, in the course of research and experimentation. Therefore, there is apparently no difference between this setting and others investigated in this book relating to the non-termination of a trance by the hypnotiser. Perry (1977) demonstrated that an uncancelled suggestion can operate post-hypnotically as well as deliberately creating posthypnotic suggestions in a subject. This means that the trance has not been thoroughly terminated, because the uncancelled suggestion is an integral part of the procedure.

There is a probable reason for this lack of reporting of adverse psychological effects upon failure to terminate a trance. It must be remembered that the laboratory setting for research and experimentation is invariably created by university and hospital qualified medical staff (more often than not in America) who are not only well versed in, but also teach hypnotic techniques and procedures. In these circumstances it is unlikely that any termination of a trance would be incomplete, or no attempt whatsoever be made to terminate. In any event there can be no doubt that the hypnotiser would be reminded by other members of the group of researchers if there were any of these omissions. This does not mean that researchers are infallible, as will be seen later in this chapter, but reports of accidental non-termination of a trances are highly unlikely to be publicised. This is particularly the case when there are likely to be nearby medical personnel immediately available to treat any adverse psychological effects which may arise. Serious adverse psychological effects are undoubtedly possible in a laboratory setting if a hypnotiser fails to terminate a hypnotic trance.

Clinical setting

Milne (1986) sets out a number of case studies in his journal article which are pertinent, but the one selected here involves failure to dehypnotise from a state of self-induced hypnosis. There is no real difference between the termination of a trance due to self-hypnosis and that of hypnosis induced by another.

Milne reports that a patient harboured a general fear of the dentist and in addition suffered from a needle phobia. He was desensitised against the fear of a dental visit and was taught how to create numbness in his jaw under self-hypnosis. Milne (1986, 17) informs us that he '[...] impressed upon the patient the importance of dehypnotising himself as soon as the treatment was ended'.

The treatment lasted over three hours and because the patient felt some pain towards the end he erroneously thought it was unnecessary to dehypnotise himself. This mistake left the patient in a complete daze for another five hours or so. Anecdotally he relates wandering around not remembering what he was doing, drove his car and became lost in his own city having no sense of direction. In addition he even forgot his own telephone number. Eventually he realised what was wrong and dehypnotised himself. Milne comments, 'The patient's instruction in dehypnotisation was clearly inadequate for such a long, drawn-out and stressful dental experience.' (p. 18).

Even though serious injury might have been easily incurred by Milne's patient it would have not, of course, qualified as an injury within the meaning of an illegal assault, because it would have been self-inflicted. However, this case of Milne's patient serves to demonstrate how an unterminated trance in a clinical setting is dangerous, even though, in this case not producing any serious psychological injury.

On stage

One can understand a stage hypnotist wanting to provide his audience with continuous entertainment and to that end, when a stage hypnotist has finished with a subject, the termination of trance is usually brief – if it exists at all – so the subject leaves the stage as quickly as possible. In these circumstances the hypnotist has little regard for the thorough and complete termination of the trance, which could result in serious adverse effects.

Kleinhauz and Beran (1984) report on a teenage girl who was not properly dehypnotised by the hypnotist before leaving the stage. Prior to leaving the theatre her friends informed the hypnotist that she felt drowsy. The hypnotist advised that she should go home to sleep when she would awaken feeling fine. However, the girl felt unwell, was hospitalised and underwent a week-long period of deep stupor. The deepest trance in the Lecron and Bordeau system for defining the depth of a trance is 'plenary' which is described as a 'Stuporous condition in which all spontaneous activity is inhibited' (see Appendix A, Part VI (p. 188)). In addition to the stupor, the girl was rigid (part of the stage performance involved her being a 'rod of steel' whilst positioned with her head on one chair and her feet on another with the hypnotist standing on her abdomen), totally unresponsive, with anosmia (loss of the sense of smell) and total anaesthesia.

Moris Kleinhauz was consulted, and he and Beran (1984, p. 285) describe what happened:

> On the seventh day, a psychiatrist (M. K.) trained in hypnotherapeutic techniques was consulted. On the assumption that she had not been properly dehypnotised, he began to intervene into her hypnotic state, and once rapport was established, succeeded in fully dehypnotising her. The techniques of hypnosis and dynamic psychotherapy were successful within one day, in returning the patient to a normal "waking" state, with full recovery of her perceptions, memory and relationship to herself and her surroundings.

Even though the girl's symptoms were relatively short-lived there can be no doubt she was injured as a result of the stage hypnotist's failure to properly terminate the trance and with her injuries being DSM-IV listed they were of a nature to qualify as part of an illegal assault.

In amateur context

In this category of the failure to terminate a hypnotic trance the reason is invariably the inexperience of the hypnotiser. Usually, the hypnotiser is a student operating on his student colleagues, either just for fun, or perhaps in an effort to settle examination nerves and improve results. Often the so-called amateur obtains his knowledge from a library book and is completely unaware of the dangers of hypnosis. One of the dangers is, of course, the failure to terminate the trance of which a precise procedure is set out in Chapter 2.

Kleinhauz and Beran (1984) again provide an example to illustrate the failure to terminate a trance when they relate how a young man was referred to a mental hospital because of his bizarre behaviour, which included drastic withdrawal from external stimuli, apathy and passivity. In addition he complained of tunnel vision, a feeling of becoming a robot and told the doctors he was a genius. He had informed the medical officers that he had been hypnotised by a friend to help him succeed with written school examinations, but the doctors ignored this information. Acute psychosis was diagnosed, but the young man's parents refused the proposed treatment and withdrew him from from the hospital. The young man asked his friend to dehypnotise him, whereupon his behaviour became normal and he functioned accordingly. It was a great pity that the doctors did not connect the symptoms to the hypnotic event. Kleinhauz and Beran (1984, p. 287) comment: 'It is possible to conclude that his symptomology had been a product of continuing hypnotic state.'

Failure of Subject to Allow Termination

Laboratory setting

In an experimental hypnotic session with a student subject Sakata (1968) found the subject had failed to dehypnotise. The hypnosis had been induced by tape recorder, with Sakata personally administering dehypnotisation procedures.

In a follow up interview the subject reported that he did not dehypnotise because he 'felt heavy and tired' and 'did not want to make the effort' to awaken. He could remember all that had occurred whilst under hypnosis except the fly hallucination test, which he failed to perform. The subject particularly remembered thinking that the taped voice reminded him of his psychology professor, which was perhaps influenced by the hypnosis session being conducted in his psychology classroom. He missed his next appointment with Sakata, but turned up three days later and complained of being unable to concentrate, having difficulty awakening and easily falling asleep in class. He was again dehypnotised and remarked that the tired feeling had gone and he felt refreshed.

In his dealings with the subject Sakata's overall impression of him included a personality where certain needs, such as dependency and submissiveness, were important features. The subject himself admitted to being very susceptible to the opinions of others.

Sakata suggests there were three reasons why the subject did not dehypnotise. One or more of the reasons can be applied to most other instances of subjects having no wish for the trance to terminate. This is, therefore, an important case study by Sakata even though, for the purpose of this guide, the adverse effects were not sufficiently serious, or of a long enough duration, to amount to injury as part of an illegal assault.

The first of Sakata's (1968, p. 224) three reasons is:

> It is conceivable that the failure of such a compliant personality in executing a suggested task could have contributed to a failure to dehypnotise because of "unfinished business", repression of the unsuccessful task after awakening, and a prolongation or reinstatement of hypnosis at a later date.

The reference to "unfinished business" is the fly hallucination test, which the subject not only failed, but initially had no memory of it being administered.

The second reason from Sakata reads:

> […] Accounting for the failure to dehypnotise is that the trance afforded a degree of relief from, or a general defense against, anxiety engendered by the general circumstances of stress operating in subject's life situation at the time of the second hypnotic session. (p. 225)

Sakata points out that the subject was under some financial burden at the time of the complications and also had expressed some concern over an impending examination. Some years previously, writing about failure to dehypnotise, Williams (1953, p. 8) had come to the same conclusion as Sakata when he stated that '[…] the trance affords a degree of relaxation […] which may also serve to avoid facing reality'.

The third reason provided by Sakata is:

> […] That S was antagonised by E's behaviour and was able to express his hostility towards E in essentially a passive-aggressive maneuver consonant with the hypnotic condition. (p. 226)

Sakata reports that even though his relationship with the subject was neutral, it may be that the subject became antagonised by his general handling of the situation, or perhaps his tardiness. Alternatively, it may be that the subject related the similar voice of his psychology professor on the tape to some unhappy memories of his studies, which caused his unwillingness to be dehypnotised.

Clinical setting

In his journal article Gravitz (1995) informs us that in therapeutic use it is rare to encounter difficulty in alerting a patient from the hypnotic condition. He continues that in over three decades of clinical experience he has only known of two instances of inability to dehypnotise.

One of the two instances involved the wife of a naval officer stationed in Japan. She chronically suffered from a neurological disorder of which one of the symptoms was severe pain, for which analgesia was ineffective, but hypnosis was successfully used to control it. Upon returning to the United States the pain returned and again medication was not helpful. Upon visiting Gravitz she proved to be a good hypnotic subject, but failed to respond to alerting instructions and continued to be in the same depth of trance. She was asked, still in the trance, how she felt and what she was thinking. She replied "Great", but said she was afraid to open her eyes. Her fear was, of course, that the pain would return upon re-establishing full consciousness and re-encountering reality, which is one of Sakata's reasons for a subject remaining in a trance. However, Gravitz allayed her fear by telling her the pain would not reoccur, whereupon she allowed herself to be dehypnotised.

Even though there were no serious adverse effects, there could well have been if the refusal to dehypnotise had not been dealt with by an experienced and qualified psychiatrist such as Gravitz.

On stage

Kleinhauz and Beran (1984) report a case involving a girl admitted to hospital with most serious adverse psychological effects after failure of trance termination. In a separate journal article of 1981 the same authors provide greater detail of the study including the fact that the defaulting stage hypnotist was called to the hospital on the second day after the girl's admission when he unsuccessfully tried to dehypnotise her. Kleinhauz and Beran (1984, p. 158) relate how:

> 'At first the girl tried to respond submissively [...]. The hypnotist's own anger, threatening posture, and shouts, however, created anxiety, anger, and fear in the patient, which she could avoid only by refusing to allow herself to be aroused.'

By this means the girl avoided confrontation with the stage hypnotist who had antagonised her.

In amateur context

Danto (1967) provides a case study of the danger of a subject unwilling to dehypnotise in an amateur context.

He reports on an 18-year-old female college student who had been placed in a trance by one of her instructors in a supermarket parking lot at night, whereupon sexual advances were made by the amateur hypnotist, which she resisted. She refused to be dehypnotised and was in a light trance for over sixteen hours and complained of a severe headache and of optic pain. Danto eventually dehypnotised the student. Her history, Danto tells us, reveals an over protective mother who lectured the girl on the "evils of sex" and discouraged her from dating unless the mother was present. The girl was sexually inhibited and on occasions when attempting to 'make out' became overwhelmed by anxiety and at times became hysterical.

Danto (1967, p. 98) advises that the girl (together with another girl mentioned in the same journal article):

> [...] Showed conflicts [...] toward their own sexual feelings. The latter conflicts appeared to be related to their resistance at being awakened from their hypnotic trances.'

This circumstance is recognised by Orne (1965, p. 229) who, apart from telling us that the refusal on the part of the subject to awaken usually '[...] Involved clandestine hypnotic experiments of students', and that this response '[...] allows the subject to express hostility towards the hypnotist [...]'.

Although the girl in the study of Danto (1967) suffered adverse effects they were not serious enough to amount to injury as part of an illegal assault, particularly with them being of a temporary nature. The study, however, demonstrates that adverse effects can, and do, arise where a subject is reluctant to be dehypnotised in an amateur context.

The hypnotiser's failure to terminate the trance, and the refusal by the subject to be dehypnotised, are real dangers in all three major hypnotic settings, as well as in the amateur context, which could generate serious adverse psychological effects which qualify as injury as part of illegal assault.

Chapter 8
Dangers of Hypnosis – Coercion

The Nature of Hypnotic Coercion

Coercion, as a risk in hypnosis, has a particular meaning in the language of hypnosis. It can be described as 'the capability of a hypnotist to compel hypnotised persons to commit dangerous, criminal (including murder and manslaughter) and immoral acts, to injure themselves and others, and generally to be of antisocial behaviour' ('improper behaviour'). Coercion in this context does not only apply to a subject in the hypnotic state, but also posthypnotically.

This is a very broad description of hypnotic coercion, but only a part is relevant to this guide, being any serious psychological injury suffered by the subject, as a result of instructions given by the hypnotist.

The important difference between coercion as a risk in hypnosis and other dangers, such as in therapeutic use, is that the former is conducted with what Karle (1991, 190) calls 'Malicious Intent', whereas adverse effects arising from the latter are assumed to be without previous and deliberate planning on the part of the hypnotist.

It is generally thought that subjects will act in whatever manner is suggested to them by a hypnotist, because they are completely under his power and as a result are unable to resist. The mass media propagate an apparent belief in the absolute control of a hypnotist over the hypnotised subject. For example, in the long running American television series of Columbo, an evil hypnotist was often depicted as having the power to coerce other characters to commit suicide by jumping off tall buildings and cliff tops. Such scenes are, of course, fictional, but one wonders if the stories of intelligence agencies (particularly of the American Central Intelligence Agency) hypnotically creating assassins might be founded in truth.

The hypnotist appears to be assisted in his mission of coercion by the very nature of hypnosis itself, which may increase the vulnerability of the subject to abuse. In Chapter 3 some of the characteristics of hypnosis were set out in the absence of an agreed definition, including increased suggestibility and reduced reality testing. It would be very easy to conclude that the reason for a subject's improper coercive behaviour is solely a result of the conducive nature of hypnosis. However, this is certainly not the case. Even the experts are divided upon the question of whether a hypnotised person can be coerced into committing acts of improper behaviour, which he or she would not commit in the fully conscious state.

Even though this danger of coercion in hypnosis is controversial, and injuries arising from it are rare, it is proper that it should be included in this book. To omit coercion would result in an incomplete examination of the risks in hypnosis.

Jacob H. Conn's Eleven Experts on Coercion

In his journal article Conn (1972) writes about the dangers of coercion in hypnosis. To obtain different views on the topic his adopted method was to write to '[…] a selected number of experts asking if a major crime could be committed under hypnosis'. He wrote to eleven so-called experts on hypnosis and it is their replies – called 'personal communications' by Conn – that are central to this chapter. Conn does not provide the full text of the personal communications, but the reader is left in no doubt which side of the coercion debate each of the experts belong.

Expert 1: E. M. Erikson

> An antisocial act has to be antisocial, it just cannot be a laboratory performance (and) you don't need hypnosis to induce antisocial behavior. In

fact hypnosis is a handicap in inducing antisocial behavior [...] anybody doing something antisocial wants to know where he is and who is around and what time of day it is and the possible consequences. Hypnosis ... constricts the awareness of surroundings and this constriction defeats efforts [...] The person would want to be fully aware and self protected as possible.

Erikson raises three interesting aspects but, before considering them an interpretation of 'self protected' is necessary. Self protection, in the sense used by Erikson, is the avoidance of the consequences of injury to oneself and others, not committing criminal or illegal acts and generally not behaving in an improper and antisocial manner.

The first of the three aspects raised by Erikson is the idea that an antisocial act is not genuinely antisocial if it takes place in a laboratory setting. Conn (1972, p. 66) informs us that Erikson refers to such acts as 'make believe'.

The 1965 experimental studies of Orne and Evans support Erikson. These studies involved twelve subjects of whom six were deeply hypnotised and the others instructed to simulate hypnosis thereby deceiving the hypnotist. All the subjects were asked to pick up a poisonous snake with their bare hands and also to throw a beaker of nitrous acid at a research assistant. The result was that five of the hypnotised subjects tried to pick up the snake, but all subjects threw the acid. (The subjects were protected from the snake by a pane of glass which was invisible to them and the research assistant was similarly protected.)

These experiments of Orne and Evans are also relevant to the second point to arise from the Eriksonian quotation and in particular his reference to not needing hypnosis to induce antisocial behaviour. However, in this circumstance there must be something else present and that 'something' is to be found within the context of the laboratory setting itself. Illustrative of this point are the Milgram (1965) studies which did not involve hypnosis.

Milgram divided his subjects into two equal groups of 'teachers' and 'learners', but in fact the teachers were the real subjects and the learners were the experimenter's stooges. The teachers were instructed to deliver increasingly higher voltage electric shocks to the learners, when they answered a question incorrectly. The shock delivering equipment was marked from low all the way up to high intensity and finally 'DANGER XXX'.

Despite the learners in an adjacent room loudly complaining, screaming, with apparent pain and begging the teacher to stop, some of the teachers continued until the learner appeared to pass out. Milgram and his assistants instructed and encouraged the subjects to keep going. The final results were that up to 66% of the subjects administered the maximum electric shock knowing the learners could die as a result.

There have been many debates upon different issues arising from the Milgram electric shock experiment. The issue relevant to coercion concerns the context of the experiment in that it took place in a university and was conducted by white coated personnel of whom some were medically qualified. The subjects thereby felt that in such circumstances neither they, nor the so-called learners, would be injured with the experiment being safe and harmless. Thus, it is not only the environment, but also the status of the persons present, which is important when subjects are coerced into carrying out antisocial, dangerous and potentially criminal acts of violence and all this without the help of hypnosis.

Likewise, in the Orne and Evans (1965) experiments the context convinced the hypnotised subjects that actions were make believe. The Orne and Evans and Milgram studies support Erikson's idea that it is pointless testing the reactions of subjects to coercive suggestions, when they perceive the context as experimental.

The third aspect Erikson raises is the subject's desire to be 'self-protected'. In Chapter 3 some of the characteristics of the nature of hypnosis were either discussed or listed. One of the listed characteristics concerned the narrowing of attention, which means the subject focuses only upon items the hypnotist suggests. Another characteristic – reality testing reduced – was fully discussed, when it was stated that a hypnotised subject uncritically accepts ideas and propositions suggested by the hypnotiser.

Superficially, these characteristics appear to be at odds with Erikson's concept of antisocial behaviour, but Erikson also feels that anyone involved in antisocial activities wants to know the full circumstances, including the possible consequences. Thus, bearing in mind the two characteristics of narrowing of attention and reality testing reduced, it makes sense when Erikson proposes that 'hypnosis … constricts the awareness of surroundings and the constriction defeats efforts [...] The person would want to be fully aware and self protected as possible.' The 'efforts' referred to are, of course, the attempts to coerce hypnotised subjects into committing acts of improper behaviour, but that is not possible, according to Erikson, when the subjects are in a completely self protected situation.

Conn (1972, p. 66) appropriately writes, based upon Erikson's personal communication, as follows:

> For a real crime or genuine antisocial behaviour, there has to be knowledge of it and intent. Such knowledge and intent brings forth self-protective behaviour.

If one accepts Erikson's views of attempted coercive improper behaviour in hypnosis there cannot be any danger which can create injury to the subject or others, but Erikson is only the first of Conn's experts.

Expert 2: R. E. Shor

> I feel quite certain that hypnosis *per se* could not be used for the purpose of committing a major crime. The idea that persons in hypnosis lose their fundamental defenses and basic moral commitments is contrary to all I know of the phenomenon.

Shor's hypnosis *per se* does not involve any manipulation, but is merely a straightforward suggestion to a subject to commit a major crime which, according to Shor, would be rejected.

Kline (1972, p. 83) also recognises that hypnosis *per se* is not sufficient to coerce improper behaviour:

> [...] It would seem the critical issue in attempting to evaluate the production of any type of transgression or antisocial behaviour cannot be viewed within the construct of hypnosis alone [...].

Shor's 'fundamental defenses' are not related to Freudian 'defence mechanisms' (see Chapter 2) but should be regarded in similar fashion to Erikson's 'self-protection'. Thus, fundamental defenses are raised in a hypnotised person, when coercive improper behaviour is suggested and as a result a person is saved from the consequences of improper behaviour.

Hans Eysenck (1970) proposed that personality traits were 'relatively enduring'. 'Morals' are represented by personality traits, which are not going to change upon a mere suggestion from a hypnotiser that a subject be of improper behaviour. So, it is easy to understand why Shor states that persons do not lose their 'basic moral commitments' in hypnosis.

Shor believes there is no prospect of injury emanating from coercive improper behaviour when hypnosis per se is involved.

Expert 3: E. R. Hilgard

> You cannot say a person will not commit a crime under hypnosis. It is another thing to say that hypnosis is alone responsible.

Once more the notion that hypnosis is a tool for creating coercive improper behaviour is rejected.

Expert 4: M. E. Wright

> [...] That a situation can be manipulated so that a trusting person is exploited, [...] This can be done in hypnosis or out of hypnosis.

Wright's emphasis is upon trust, also features in the Orne and Evans (1965) and Milgram (1965) studies, to the extent that the subjects trusted the experimenters to ensure that they would not come to any harm.

However, Wright's personal communication is of a more general nature and includes other relationships in nonlaboratory settings, such as, medical advisor and patient, solicitor and client and clergyman and a member of his flock. Within these relationships there is a built-in element of trust on the part of the lay person, to the extent that the law recognises such lay persons can be unduly influenced by their advisor.

Karle's report (1991, p. 191) illustrates the trust operating in a clinical setting. Karle was the Principal Psychologist at Guys Hospital, London. He relates how a female patient, who had previously been treated by a hypnotherapist, sought his help. She informed him that upon her first appointment with a hypnotherapist he had induced her to undress and on the second and subsequent meetings sexual intercourse had taken place. The hypnotherapist had advised her that all her problems stemmed from sexual inhibition and her 'treatment' was designed to free her from this underlying cause. It seems that she trusted the hypnotherapist and accepted the treatment which she otherwise might not have considered.

Expert 5: H. B. Crasilneck

> A person could be hypnotised into committing an antisocial act, providing they were an excellent subject, and if they were hallucinated to the fact, that the act was acceptable to their own unconscious mind.

Crasilneck's reference to a person being an excellent subject must be interpreted in accordance with the Lecron and Bordeau system for defining the depth of a trance (see Appendix A, Part VI, p. 188). These symptoms reveal the depth of the trance as 'deep or somnambulistic' which is not often achieved in hypnotised persons (see Chapter 2). In psychology factors that determine what is perception include hallucinations and perceptual distortions which are regarded as being of the same psychological category. Reber advises:

> Distortion and hallucination. Strong emotional feelings can distort perceptions rather dramatically and hallucinations can be produced by a variety of causes [...] These 'misperceptions' are an intriguing problem because the essential perception seems to come from 'inside the head' rather than the environment.

The hallucinations referred to in Chapter 3, as part of one of the characteristic of hypnosis, arise naturally, but Crasilneck's hallucinations and Schneck's perceptual distortions are manufactured by the hypnotist.

Reber's so-called misperceptions in psychology are reflected in hypnosis, in that artefactual hallucinations and perceptual distortions are joined together, with no attempt being made to distinguish them, even though there is a difference. Hallucinations are completely 'inside the head' whereas perceptual distortions, whilst still inside the head, are related to a physical presence. In practice, the difference is of no consequence.

Scheflin *et al* (1989, p. 137) endorse Crasilneck's view: 'To expect that a person [...] would become a killer simply because a hypnotist ordered it is absurd.' However, they continue by providing a hypothetical example of a hypnotist convincing a subject that his or her child was in danger from a stranger when they warn '[...] the person's desire to protect the child could have serious consequences'.

Perry (1979, p. 187) states:

> [...] That coercion is possible through the induction of distorted perceptions which delude the hypnotized person into believing that behaviour suggested is not transgressive.

In the course of a short review of experimental and clinical findings, concerning antisocial and criminal acts induced by hypnosis, Barber (1961) analyses an experiment by Watkins (1947). The experiment involved a deeply hypnotised army private being induced to believe that a senior officer was a Japanese soldier, whom he had to kill by strangulation. The Private had to be pulled off the senior officer who he really thought, by virtue of induced misperception, was a Japanese soldier who must be killed. Barber suggests other explanations for the Private's behaviour, such as the experimenter stating he would be responsible for any consequences of the subject's behaviour.

In a later journal Watkins (1972, p. 95) writes:

> If it (hypnosis) is potent enough to initiate constructive behaviour, it is sufficiently powerful to alter psychic balance in antisocial directions in the hands of an unscrupulous operator. [Brackets added.]

This alteration of psychic balance, referred to by Watkins, includes induced misperceptions.

Despite extensive research no reports of coercive improper behaviour involving misperceptions, other than in an experimental setting have been found. However, in view of what the experts say, it seems likely that a hypnotised person might be induced into committing acts of improper behaviour in a natural setting. As a result injury could be caused, directly or indirectly, to self and others.

Expert 6: J. M. Schneck

> […] Is of the opinion that a major crime can be committed by a hypnotic subject […] if the subject were unaware that he is participating in a crime (after induced perceptual distortion) […]

Schneck is only believes that a subject can commit a major crime, and even then only with the assistance of induced perceptual distortion, in other words, a misperception.

Expert 7: L. R. Wolberg

> […] That relatively few people may be induced to commit a crime or perpetrate antisocial acts even when they are themselves criminally inclined or antisocial. They will do so in or out of hypnosis when it satisfies an important need in themselves.

Wolberg restricts the people who 'may be induced to commit a crime or perpetrate antisocial acts' to those few who have an internal need to satisfy. This internal need to satisfy that part of the brain which craves psychological need-gratification (such as the excitement found when experiencing danger or the fear of being apprehended) is presumably generated when committing a serious crime. Alternatively, it could be satisfying an economic need.

Wolberg states that those persons who fit into his specified class of persons will commit acts of improper behaviour in or out of hypnosis.

Expert 8: G. W. Williams

> The evidence in such cases is circumstantial and opinions are antiquated
> … If a stable person is hypnotised and told to commit a crime it is my opin-
> ion that he would reject the suggestion.

Williams could not be clearer in his assessment of the prospect of a
hypnotised person being coerced into committing a crime. His
only reservation is in a laboratory setting, about which he goes on
to state: 'Laboratory crimes have innumerable parameters which
weaken or invalidate an opinion of a positive connection.'

Expert 9: H. Spiegal

> I have no doubt that hypnosis can be used to encourage another to commit
> a crime … Although it is possible for the subject to ultimately resist a post-
> hypnotic signal, there is a varying time factor before the correction can
> occur. It is during this transition that the momentum of the hypnotic influ-
> ence is still present. Conn (1972, p. 67).

Spiegal clearly believes that hypnosis can be used to 'encourage'
another to commit a crime.

The only concern of Spiegal is the period of time the 'hypnotic
influence' is sustained. He points out that the influence continues
until it is posthypnotically rejected.

Expert 10: B. B. Raginsky

> Crime could be committed given the right kind of personality make-up
> with the subject, the timing of the suggestion, the ability of the hypnotizer
> to have the subject fantasize a situation where the crime would seem a nat-
> ural procedure for that particular person under these conditions.

Raginsky mentions having the subject 'fantasize'. Reber defines
fantasy as, 'A term generally used to refer the mental process of
imagining objects, symbols or events not immediately present.' It
is likely that fantasy can be placed in the same category as
Crasilneck and Schneck's misperceptions and treated accordingly.

Provided all the conditions which Raginsky specifies are present his view is that a person could commit a crime under, and as a result of, hypnosis. It must follow that such a person could also be of improper behaviour generally, from which injury could arise.

Expert 11: J. Lassner

> [...] Hypnosis has been involved in criminal acts committed by the hyp-notised person on the instigation of the hypnotist. [...] It seems to me that hypnosis was only invoked in order to escape blame or punishment.

Lassner feels that there can be no injury arising from coercion because the alleged hypnotic trance was a charade and was per-haps being raised as a defence of automatism to criminal activity.

Evaluation of Coercion as a Danger of Hypnosis

Out of all the opinions expressed by Conn's eleven experts and others cited above, only one real life case (i.e. outside the labora-tory setting) showed that improper behaviour might be hypnoti-cally induced. The case involved a trusting female hypnotherapy client. However, it was generally agreed that a trusting relation-ship can be abused both in and out of hypnosis.

Perry's (1979) review of an Australian court case reveals how even though admitting sexual intercourse with various hypnotised female clients, a hypnotist was found not guilty. Five experts gave evidence that the clients need not have lost control over their actions and were no more likely to carry out the requested behav-iour because of being hypnotised. Gordon Milne, a famed Australian psychologist, agreed with the court decision and wrote about what he called 'hypnotic compliance' as, '[...] peculiar to the use of hypnosis is a fallacious belief in the power it enables the operator to wield over the subject' (1986, p. 15).

In a paper published in 1981, Conn wrote:

> Coercion through hypnosis is a myth which will not disappear so long as
> it is fostered by uninformed hypnotists, who believe that all initiative and
> self-determination is surrendered by the subject to an "all powerful"
> hypnotist.

In view of the above Perry court case review, the two quotations
from Milne and Conn, some of Conn's eleven experts and others
cited earlier in this chapter, it seems unlikely that a hypnotised person could be coerced in real life into behaving improperly.
However, it cannot be said with absolute certainty that it could
never arise other than in the laboratory context, particularly considering the opinions of Conn's experts such as Crasilneck and
Schneck. Therefore, while a doubt exists, it is proper that the coercion debate should be explored in the pursuit of injury as part of
an illegal assault.

Chapter 9

Dangers of Hypnosis –
Performance on Stage

Kost (1965, 220) sums up the risks of hypnosis in general, and hypnosis used for entertainment in particular, as:

> The dangers that are involved in hypnosis occur through ignorance,
> overzealousness, lack of understanding of the bases of interpersonal rela-
> tionships, and the irresponsible acts of those who would use the technique
> for entertainment.

Kost is clearly referring to stage hypnotists who use hypnotic techniques for the entertainment of an audience.

Stage hypnosis invariably involves a number of people in a trance at the same time, takes place in front of a paying audience in a theatre, or on television, and is designed for entertainment purposes. Experimental hypnosis is used for research purposes, usually by qualified medical personnel with hypnosis training and experience, involves one subject or a group of subjects and is conducted in laboratory conditions in accordance with a predetermined design. Clinical hypnosis is typically performed by a professional, usually upon one client in a private quiet place and is used for therapeutic purposes.

The contrasting circumstances of stage hypnosis results in differences in the experience and behaviours of a subject and the effects of a hypnotic trance. Some of the differences and commonalties have already been mentioned earlier. One commonalty is the risk resulting from pre-existing conditions.

Pre-existing Conditions and Stage Hypnosis

It was explained in Chapter 4 that a subject may have what this author has called a 'pre-existing condition'. A pre-existing condition could be either a physical or mental ailment already present, latently or manifestly, in the subject prior to hypnosis.

A prudent clinician would enquire into a client's medical history, with particular reference to pre-existing conditions, and act accordingly, a stage hypnotist does not have the time or opportunity to do this. Furthermore, a subject may be taking prescribed drugs, such as tranquillisers or antidepressants, of which the stage hypnotist knows nothing, with the possible consequence of the subject abreacting upon the induction of a trance.

The point is that even if the induction of a trance inter-reacts with a pre-existing condition, or with prescribed drugs, and adverse effects arise, it cannot be said that the hypnosis was the cause. This situation is not just peculiar to stage hypnosis, but it is equally applicable to both experimental and clinical settings. However, it will be remembered that even though adverse effects arose in the experimental settings of Hilgard (1974) and Judd *et al* (1985) there were no injuries qualifying as part of an illegal assault (see Chapter 5). It was, therefore, suggested that serious injuries were unlikely to be associated with hypnosis in a laboratory context. Clinical settings are a separate case because all categories of pre-existing conditions considered in Chapter 4 are clinically applicable.

Kleinhauz, Dreyfuss, Beran, Goldberg and Azikri (1979) write:

> Hypnosis, *per se*, is a precipitating factor which may trigger psychopatho-
> logical manifestations. These manifestations may include spontaneous
> abreaction, acute anxiety states during the trance, difficulties in dehypno-
> tising, and the appearance of a long uncontrolled trance. (p. 219)

In the case of *Gates v McKenna* (see 'Danger of precipitating a mental disorder' in Chapter 4) the plaintiff did not succeed in his claim for damages against McKenna, the stage hypnotist, in respect of allegedly causing his schizophrenia. The court considered that his latent mental disorder was 'triggered' by the hypnosis and not caused by it. This reported court case is the only English case, involving alleged adverse psychological effects found to date, despite extensive and thorough research.

It can be confidently stated that the one relevant pre-existing condition of precipitating a mental disorder may be discounted when considering injury arising from stage hypnosis. It is important to eliminate pre-existing conditions which as a result goes some way to being able to consider the effect of hypnosis *per se*.

Hypnosis **per se** *in Stage Entertainment*

There is no evidence to support the hypothesis that hypnosis induced upon a stage – with no therapeutic element and pre-existing condition involvement – is associated with *any* adverse effects which amount to injury forming part of an illegal assault.

The case of *Gates v McKenna* indirectly supports the view that hypnosis alone – for example, applied in a laboratory setting (see Chapter 6) – will not cause serious adverse effects, but are almost certainly due to a combination of hypnosis and therapies, or pre-existing conditions.

Failure to Dehypnotise in Stage Entertainment

One of Echterling's (1988, 279) differences which can produce serious adverse psychological effects, and to which he obliquely alludes when he writes:

> The stage hypnotist sets aside little or no time for dehypnosis and debriefing. [...] Hypnotic subjects often reported that they were disappointed that the stage hypnotist was unavailable immediately after the performance to answer their questions and help them process their experience.

In Echterling & Emmerling (1987) the authors write:

> [...] The stage hypnotist rarely is available to hypnotic subjects who might experience adverse reactions later. Unfortunately, too often stage hypnotists follow a "hit-and-run" approach and are quickly on their way to their next scheduled performance. (pp. 153–4)

To summarise the danger of stage hypnosis it can be confidently stated that, excluding adverse effects related to pre-existing conditions and the unlikelihood of them arising from hypnosis *per se*, there is only one source of danger which is failure to dehypnotise.

Kost's (1965, p. 220) reference at the beginning of this chapter to, '[...] the irresponsible acts of those who would use the technique for entertainment' is certainly true of those hypnotists who fail to terminate a trance, or cause a subject to resist returning to a conscious state.

Chapter 10

Criminal Assault

Elements of a Crime

The criminal courts are empowered to punish those defendants whose conduct violates the law by constituting, threatening or causing a harmful result. No matter if harm is occasioned to a person, say, in the course of robbery, by way of financial loss, physical injury in a night club brawl or psychological harm caused by an assault.

In all cases of harmful conduct the conditions must be such that blame attaches to the defendant with it being accepted that there are two applicable conditions. They are, first, a harmful act (called *'actus reus'*) with an accompanying mental element (called *'mens rea'*) and, second, the defendant does not have a valid defence

Therefore, there are three elements of a crime – *actus reus, mens rea* (unless otherwise stated by statute) and the absence of a valid defence, in order for a defendant to be convicted of a criminal offence. This chapter will be examining the first two of the elements, as the basis for discussion of the various forms of criminal assault, in relation to injuries arising from the dangers of hypnosis. The third element speaks for itself.

Hypnosis, Injury and Criminal Assault

In Chapter 4 of this book the nature of psychological injury as part of an illegal assault was discussed, when a benchmark for distinguishing serious psychological injuries from injuries of a non-serious or transient nature was established. It was suggested that the adverse psychological effects associated with hypnosis would qualify as injury – within the meaning of illegal assault – if they were contained in the DSM-IV. A list of these serious injuries is set out in Part I of Appendix B (p. 191). It was further suggested that neither the less serious injuries, such as ordinary everyday headaches, dizziness and nausea, nor those injuries of a transient nature, do not amount to qualifying injuries.

MacHovec (1986) assisted with the distinction in his comprehensive list of 'complications' associated with hypnosis (see Part II, Appendix B (p. 193)), which have been divided in serious injury (in the sense of being DSM-IV listed) and nonserious injury in this book. The former qualify as injury for the purpose of illegal assault (meaning contrary to criminal law and also as the tort of assault and battery at civil law) and the latter do not.

There are three major settings in which hypnosis is applied: in a laboratory for research and experimental reasons; at a private place for therapeutic purposes; and on the stage for the entertainment of the public. The adverse effects arising in the laboratory setting were of a minor and transient nature (see Chapter 6). Surprisingly, it was found that adverse effects associated with stage hypnosis were also not serious, with both of these settings not being normally associated with adverse effects amounting to injury as listed in DSM-IV (see Chapter 9).

However, it was discovered that hypnosis, combined with therapeutic applications, can produce serious adverse effects of the type listed in DSM-IV (see Chapter 6). MacHovec's list of complications, compiled after many years in practice by him, other psychologists and hypnotherapists whilst therapeutically treating thousands of clinical patients, reflects this situation.

This does not mean that hypnosis in therapeutic use contains the only danger of serious injury. Far from it, serious adverse effects amounting to injury in illegal assault were encountered in all three major settings when the subject failed to dehypnotise (see Chapter 7). The failure of trance termination can arise where inadequate termination procedures, if any at all, are employed by the hypnotiser and also when the subject has no wish to return to the full conscious waking state due to the antagonistic attitude of the hypnotiser.

There are two key areas of risk for hypnotists in terms of DSM-IV-listed injury, as part of criminal assault. Those injuries arising from therapeutic use in a clinical setting and to certain cases of the non-termination of a trance in all three major settings.

Actus reus

Actus reus is from the Latin and means 'guilty act'. It is one of the essential elements of a crime, which a prosecutor must prove is present to secure a conviction. The guilty act means that prior to the criminal courts being interested there must be some physical act, which is either known as a 'conduct crime', or a 'result crime'. Furthermore, as Clarkson and Keating (1998, p. 95) advise, '[...] the act be carried out in legally relevant circumstances'.

Conduct crime only requires prohibited conduct itself to be present, as is found, for example, in the offence of dangerous driving. Result crime category contains a prohibited result, or consequence such as is found in the offence of causing death by dangerous driving. Causing the death of another person is, of course, the result and the offence of dangerous driving in the conduct crime.

Result crime requires the establishment of the fact that the physical conduct *caused* the illegal consequence. Physical contact is not a requirement, but physical conduct, such as driving the motor vehicle, is sufficient. In hypnosis, the act of induction and subsequent proceedings can be likened to a person quietly creeping up behind you, admiring the view on the edge of a cliff top, and loudly shouting "Boo," causing you to jump up and fall off the cliff. The physical element is that part of the human anatomy that produces speech, including the larynx, lungs, tongue and vocal chords.

Whether hypnosis is identifiable and capable of *causing* injury are the next ingredients of *actus reus* to be considered. It seems likely that, despite the lack of a consensual definition of the nature of hypnosis, a court would accept a description of its characteristics instead. In the criminal courts, a common sense approach would no doubt be adopted in identifying hypnosis as an implement causing injury. This approach may be on the basis that the court would ask itself – if it were not for the induction of a hypnotic trance, of which the characteristics are proven, would the injuries have arisen? The answer to this question would, of course, be no. In other words the court would decide that injuries were capable of being caused by hypnosis as a result of a voluntary physical act on the part of the hypnotist. As a result, another constituent element of *actus reus*, of hypnosis being capable of causing injury, would be satisfied.

It is important to locate the voluntary physical act (i.e. the *actus reus*) in the hypnotic proceedings particularly when one considers the relationship between *actus reus* and *mens rea*.

The voluntary physical act of the hypnotiser's therapeutic application is the *actus reus* which causes the injury. The other circumstance associated with serious injury is nontermination of a hypnotic trance, when the hypnotiser fails to properly and thoroughly terminate the trance. Here, the *actus reus* is the inadequate or improper application of the termination procedure which causes the injury. Where the hypnotiser makes no attempt to terminate the trance the *actus reus* must date back to the induction of the trance. In the event of the hypnotiser's aggressive attitude resulting in the subject's refusal to dehypnotise, it is the physical act of aggression which is the *actus reus* from which injury can arise.

It can be seen in each of the above circumstances where serious injury may arise that the physical conduct of the hypnotiser (in the form proposed earlier) is responsible and forms part of the definition of *actus reus*. However, in addition to the *actus reus* to secure a conviction the mental element must also be present, or deemed to be present.

Mens rea

Mens rea means a guilty mind. It is a matter for the prosecution to prove this state of mind existed at the time the accused committed the alleged offence and also, that it was present at the same time as the *actus reus* of the crime (coincidence of *actus reus* and *mens rea*). It is, therefore, open to a defendant to show he did not have *mens rea* in connection with the offence in respect of which he is charged.

Mens rea arises either by the statute which created the crime, or by precedent, which is a judgement, or part of a judgement, of a higher court used as an authority in subsequent cases in a lower court. There are three common and relevant examples of mens rea in criminal law in which this practice guide is interested, and they are: an intention to bring about a particular consequence; recklessness as to whether such consequence may arise; and negligence.

Some crimes do not require *mens rea* and are known as crimes of 'strict liability'. They include road traffic offences and offences related to food production, but not of assault. In common with all other crimes, the absence of *mens rea* because of an ignorance of the law is not a defence, nor is a good motive possessed by the defendant when committing a criminal offence. However, this does not mean a defendant cannot admit the presence of *mens rea*, but still defend the charge upon the ground, for example, of duress, in the sense that he or she was compelled to commit the offence by another person, or by surrounding circumstances.

The three aspects of *mens rea*

* intention
* recklessness
* negligence

are now discussed with particular reference to their applicability to criminal assault and hypnosis.

Intention

Although accurate it is an over simplification for Martin (1994, p. 205) in *A Dictionary of Law* to define 'intention', as a form of *mens rea* in criminal law, as, 'The state of mind of one who aims to bring about a particular consequence.'

While there is no consensus in law upon the meaning of intention, Clarkson and Keating (1998) set out three views that the courts have accepted as representing the term 'intention':

(1) 'A consequence is intended when it is the aim or objective of the actor.'
The 'actor' is, of course, accused in a criminal trial. Often this view is
referred to as 'direct intent'.

For example: A points a loaded gun at B, whom he wants to slay,
deliberately pulls the trigger and kills him. It could not be denied
by A that his intention was to murder B. Intention is therefore a
purely subjective concept in that it is not concerned with what a
reasonable person would have intended in the same circumstances, but only what the defendant was intending at the time of
the offence. Therefore, direct intent corresponds with the ordinary
and every day use of the term.

Prior to the Criminal Justice Act 1967 the law was not entirely clear
on this point of subjectivity. However, Section 8 of the Act provides
that a person is not to be regarded as having intended or foreseen
the natural and probable consequences of an act simply because
they were natural and probable, but this may be evidence from
which the court or jury may infer it was intended. Therefore, the
crucial test is what the defendant actually foresaw or intended, not
what he or she should have foreseen or intended and thereby a
subjective test of intention.

Illustrative of this subjectivity is the House of Lords appeal case of
R v Moloney [1985]:

(2) 'A consequence is intended when it is the aim or objective of the actor,
or is foreseen as a *virtual, practical* or *moral certainty* .' It is often referred to
as an 'oblique intention'.

In this well-known and often cited case the defendant, Moloney,
was convicted of the murder of his stepfather. Following a heavy
drinking session the two decided to find out who was quicker on
the draw using a shotgun. Moloney told the court that: "I didn't
aim the gun. I just pulled the trigger and he was dead." The trial
judge directed the jury that the defendant had the necessary intention to kill, "when he foresees that it will probably happen,
whether he desires it or not". The Court of Appeal supported the
trial judge, but Lord Bridge of Harwich, in his House of Lords leading judgement, which revolved around Moloney's intent, stated:

"[...] By reference to foresight of consequences, I do not believe for the judge to do more than invite the jury to consider two questions. First, was death or really serious injury in a murder case (or what ever relevant consequence must be proved to have been intended in any other case) a natural consequence of the defendant's voluntary act? Secondly, did the defendant foresee that consequence as being a natural consequence of his act? The jury should then be told that if they answer yes to both questions it is a proper inference for them to draw that he intended that consequence."

Moloney's appeal was allowed on the basis that a jury would not answer 'yes' to both the questions posed by Lord Bridge. This part of Lord Bridge's judgement was deliberately extended by him to include cases other than murder.

(3) 'A consequence is intended when it is the aim or objective of the actor or is foreseen as certain to result.'

The reference to foresight in this third view is not intention, but is merely evidence from which intention may be inferred. In *R v Hancock and Shankland* [1986] two striking miners attempted to stop other miners breaking the strike by dropping a concrete block from a bridge on to a taxi carrying them. The driver was killed and the defendants were convicted of murder. The defendants gave evidence that it was only their intention to frighten the other miners by dropping the block on the middle of the road, when they thought the taxi would be in the near side lane. In an appeal to the House of Lords, Lord Scarman stated, upon reducing the sentences from murder to manslaughter:

"[...] The greater the probability of a consequence, the more likely it is that the consequence was foreseen and if that consequence was foreseen the greater the probability is that the consequence was also intended [...]."

Lord Scarman's judgement means that even if there were overwhelming odds against a consequence being foreseen, it could still mean that death was a natural consequence of the defendants' act, but with such a degree of unlikelihood there would be little, or no evidence of intention. Thus, if one person stabs another in the chest and injury, or even death results it is highly likely that such a consequence would have been foreseen by the aggressor and, as a result, this foresight is evidence of intention. However, if a person cuts another's hand, resulting in septicaemia or tetanus and dies, even though death is a natural consequence of inflicting the initial injury, the chances of foreseeing the death are so minuscule that the lack of foresight would mean that the death was not intended.

Intention as a form of *mens rea*, from Clarkson et al's three viewpoints, can be applied to a hypnotiser and the subject of a hypnotic trance where serious injury may arise.

Clearly, it is not the direct of a hypnotiser to use the application of therapies as an implement causing injury to a subject. Likewise, in respect of injury associated with the non-termination of a trance where the hypnotiser is in default.

It is, of course, a complete contradiction of the concept of hypnotic therapy for a hypnotiser to have an intention of harming a client. On the contrary, it is the undoubted intention of the operator to be ameliorate of the subject's ill health, or to effect a beneficial change in the subject's behaviour.

Applying Clarkson *et al's* (1998) second view (oblique intention) to the same two circumstances of a therapeutic setting and failure to dehypnotise, produces a similar result to that of direct intention discussed above. Clarkson *et al's* oblique intention regards a consequence (i.e. a DSM-IV listed injury) as intended when it is either a direct intention (see above), or when it is foreseen '[...] as a *virtual, practical* or *moral certainty*' (p. 131).

In Moloney's case set out earlier, Lord Bridge stated that two questions were to be asked of the defendant's voluntary act in respect of foresight of a consequence. Extrapolating the first question one must ask is whether an injury arising from the hypnotiser's voluntary act is a natural consequence of that act. The answer is yes on the basis that if it were not for the application of a therapy, failure to adopt proper termination procedures, making no attempt whatsoever to terminate a trance, or refusal to dehypnotise due to the hypnotiser's aggressive attitude (i.e. the *actus reus*) there would be no question of injury arising and, therefore, a natural consequence of the acts of the hypnotist.

The second of Lord Bridge's extrapolated questions is whether the hypnotiser foresaw injury as a natural consequence of his act.

Again, as with direct intention, the hypnotiser would not foresee injury as a consequence arising from a voluntary act, particularly if this is coupled with Clarkson *et al*'s 'virtual, practical moral certainty'. On the contrary, in a therapeutic setting, the hypnotiser would only foresee an improvement in the subject's health or behaviour. Furthermore, in all three major settings the hypnotiser would not foresee the failure to effectively terminate the hypnotic trance as giving rise to injury. The induction process is merely being reversed, with the intention of returning the subject to status quo and injury would not be foreseen as a natural consequence. Even in the case of the hypnotiser making no attempt whatsoever to terminate the trance the omission would not have been foreseen as a virtual, practical or moral certainty as giving rise to injury. Likewise, the aggressive attitude of the hypnotiser causing the subject's refusal to dehypnotise.

The answers to the two questions posed by Lord Bridge in hypnotic circumstances are 'yes' to the first question and 'no' to the second. Therefore, it must follow that intention, as a form of *mens rea*, is not applicable. In Clarkson *et al*'s third view the consequence is worded as to be 'foreseen as certain to result'. For injury to be foreseen as certain to result there would have to be injuries arising in all cases of hypnotherapy and upon all terminations of trances. There are many studies disputing this proposition, including that of Auerback (1962) (see Chapter 5) where untoward results were experienced in their patients by only a very small minority of the 414 reporting psychiatrists, particularly those untoward results amounting to DSM-IV listed injury. Therefore, the likelihood of injury arising in these specified circumstances is so remote that there can be no evidence of intention.

However, because intention, as a form of *mens rea*, is not applicable to a hypnotist and subject in the manner described, it does not automatically mean that a hypnotist cannot be possessed of another form *mens rea*, such as 'recklessness' or 'negligence'.

Recklessness

There are two forms of recklessness in terms of *mens rea* and both bear the name of the cases in which they were defined. The cases were *R v Cunningham* [1957] and *MPC v Caldwell* [1982]. While the legal definition is similar to the ordinary everyday meaning of the word (i.e. taking an unjustifiable risk) it is more detailed and refined, and encompasses both a subjective and objective state of mind of the accused. In the current context 'subjective' means the accused's own standards or mental state by which he is judged and, by way of contrast, 'objective' means the standards or mental state of a reasonable person.

Cunningham recklessness applies what is a subjective test. In this case Cunningham broke into a gas meter to steal money. Gas escaped and seeped through into the house next door, where his prospective mother-in-law was asleep, and made her ill. Cunningham was convicted of 'maliciously administering a noxious thing so as to endanger life' contrary to Section 3 of the Offences Against the Person Act 1861. He appealed and the Court of Appeal stated that 'maliciously' meant intentionally or recklessly. The same court defined recklessness as the conscious running of an unjustifiable risk. Thus, Cunningham would have been reckless and deemed to be of *mens rea* if he thought there was a risk of a gas escape thereby endangering another person, but went ahead regardless. Cunningham's conviction was quashed, but upon a technicality involving a misdirection at the original trial.

The definition was not only followed in subsequent cases, but also became more refined, as is reflected in the case of *R v Stephenson* [1979]. In this case the subjective approach imposed two tests of recklessness, which are reported by Clarkson and Keating (1998, 156) as follows:

(1) whether the defendant foresaw the possibility of the consequence occurring; and
(2) whether it was unjustifiable or unreasonable to take the risk.

The first subjective test of recklessness simply means that an accused must have had the foresight that harm might occur, but went ahead anyway.

The Cunningham second test concerns the justifiability or reasonableness of taking a risk. This can depend on the social importance of the act of the accused, which is an aspect of recklessness as a form of *mens rea* little mentioned in the text books, but it is of considerable importance in this book.

The Law Commission, an influential independent body established by Parliament in 1965 to keep the law of England and Wales under review and to recommend reform, is of great help. In a Consultation Paper, entitled 'Codification of the Criminal Law: General Principles: Mental Element in Crime', it advised (1970, pp. 53–4):

> The second part of the definition requires that the defendant should have acted unreasonably in taking the risk. The inquiry as to the reasonableness of his conduct will involve a number of factors, amongst which will be the social importance or otherwise of what he was doing. The operation of public transport, for example, is inevitably accompanied by risks of the operator, yet it is socially necessary that these risks be taken. Dangerous surgical operations must be carried out in the interests of the life and health of the patient, yet the taking of these risks is socially justifiable, On the other hand, the social benefit achieved by keeping an appointment to the minute does not justify the taking of foreseen risks of accidents which may be caused by driving dangerously in particular circumstances.

Lord Justice Lane, in the *R v Stephenson* case, no doubt had something similar in mind when he stated:

> "It is however not the taking of every risk which could be properly classed as reckless. The risk must be one which it is in all the circumstances unreasonable for him to take."

The onus is placed on the person proposing to take a risk to assess the chances of harm arising, whilst taking into account the social usefulness of the activity, and also the seriousness, or otherwise, of the harm. If, for example, in the above Law Commission reference to public transport, there is one chance in thirty train journeys of an accident occurring where serious injury could be caused, taking that risk is clearly unjustifiable. However, the same chance in thirty, or even less, applied to a complicated and life saving surgical operation could be justified and the risk taken regarded as reasonable.

The first test of recklessness mentioned above in connection with Cunningham recklessness, whilst remaining as a Cunningham test, was substantially changed by the House of Lords in *MPC v*

Caldwell when it created the new and additional test of so-called Caldwell-type recklessness.

The problem of having two separate tests of recklessness (i.e. Cunningham and Caldwell) is to decide which test of recklessness to apply to different offences. Fortunately, where criminal assault is concerned, the problem was resolved in the case of *R v Spratt* [1991] when it was held that Cunningham recklessness applied to all assault offences. However, for completeness the Caldwell-type recklessness is briefly mentioned, which Card, Cross and Jones (1998, 59) express in general terms, based upon the judgement of Lord Diplock, as follows:

> A person is Caldwell-type reckless as to a particular risk which attends his conduct if that risk is obvious and either:
>
> (1)   he has not given any thought to the possibility of there being any such risk; or
>
> (2)   he has recognised that there is some risk involved and has nevertheless persisted in his conduct.

A person is guilty of reckless conduct in (2) above where there is 'some risk' involved, which means that even a slight or remote risk is within Lord Diplock's model direction of recklessness. This means that the largely objective tests of Caldwell-type recklessness are not as strict as the subjective Cunningham tests.

The question now to be asked is whether recklessness, as a form of *mens rea*, could apply to injury arising in the circumstances of the therapeutic setting and nontermination of a hypnotic trance.

Upon applying the Cunningham tests of recklessness to the therapeutic setting it must be first considered if the hypnotherapist had the foresight that injury might arise. It was decided earlier that this foresight is part of the coincidence of *actus reus* and *mens rea* and occurs where a therapy is applied.

A risk exists, no matter how remote, of serious injury arising upon the application of a therapy. However, it would not be known without a detailed study of the dangers of hypnosis. A person practising hypnotherapy might think that there may be some sort of danger when a hypnotic trance is induced. But it is unlikely that such persons would perceive that injury could arise upon the application of therapy under hypnosis. However, for the purpose of this examination of recklessness, as a form of *mens rea*, one must assume that some therapists are aware of the danger. (This is where one can see the subjectiveness of the Cunningham test.)

Upon applying the second test of Cunningham recklessness, one must consider whether the application of hypnotic therapy is justifiable or reasonable, if it is known to the hypnotiser that a risk of serious injury could arise in the circumstances of the first test. This is where the social importance of hypnotic therapy is to be considered. There can be no doubt that the hypnotist's conduct in applying therapies is of social importance, whether it be to stop the subject smoking, desensitisation relating to a phobia, alleviating hay fever, or any one of the dozens of other therapies.

Before one can say it is reasonable to take a risk upon the application of a therapy it is necessary to consider the degree of risk involved.

Despite the considerable research into the dangers of hypnosis, in a therapeutic setting, it has not been possible to obtain sufficient and precise data to afford a statistically evaluate the occurrence of serious injury (that is DSM-IV listed) arising in that setting. However, serious injury, associated with the therapeutic setting, although not rare would seem to arise most infrequently (for example, see Auerback (1962), Judd, *et al.* (1986), Levitt, *et al.* (1962) and Chapter 5.

The seriousness of the injury which might result must also be taken into account when assessing the degree of risk involved. For example, if death might be the outcome of the application of a hypnotic therapy the risk is obviously not worth taking, even if the therapy is for the betterment of the subject's health. However, there have been no reports of death from any of the risks of hypnosis, but there have been some fairly serious psychological injuries arising that are listed in DSM-IV and by McHovec (1988) and which are set out in Parts I and II of Appendix B (pp. 191 and 193).

Upon the basis that hypnotic therapy is socially useful, it can be safely stated that the extremely low chance of serious harm arising it does not amount to recklessness, as a form of *mens rea*. It follows that even though recklessness may be present according to the first Cunningham test, it can be negated by the second social usefulness test.

In respect of the other circumstance where serious injury may arise, failure to dehypnotise the subject is to be found in all three major settings (see Chapter 7, p. 77). The causes are the failure of the operator to properly and thoroughly terminate the hypnotic trance, the operator making no attempt whatsoever to terminate and the refusal by the subject to return to the full waking state due to the aggressive attitude of the hypnotiser.

It must be within the knowledge of every hypnotiser in all three major settings that it is most important to properly and thoroughly terminate a trance (see Chapters 2 and 7) otherwise adverse effects could arise. This must be the case even for a hypnotist receiving the briefest training. Clearly, being possessed of this knowledge, the hypnotist must foresee that there is a risk of injury which could arise from non-termination. The hypnotist going ahead anyway means a risk has been taken and this could amount to Cunningham recklessness as a form *mens rea*. The question of social usefulness is not, of course, relevant as it was above when applying a therapy.

Where no attempt whatsoever is made to terminate, the coincidence of *actus reus* and *mens rea* is upon the induction of the hypnotic trance. At that time the hypnotist must have foreseen that a lack of termination procedure could be a risk leading to serious adverse effects.

The last of the circumstances concerning non-termination is the refusal of the subject to dehypnotise as a result of the hypnotiser's aggressive attitude. However, the majority, if not nearly all, hypnotherapists and stage hypnotists would not be aware is a risk that could give rise to serious injury. This means that those few with this specialist knowledge are possessed of *mens rea* in the form of recklessness, because they are of the foresight that the adoption of an aggressive attitude could lead to failure to dehypnotise.

After many years experience in the criminal courts as both a prosecuting solicitor and defender in private practice, I am of the firm opinion that the prosecuting authorities would not be interested in taking a hypnotiser before the criminal courts in the circumstance of a subject refusing to dehypnotise, as a result of a hypnotiser's aggressive attitude. It would not only be most difficult, if not impossible, to prove the foresight and the aggressive attitude, but also to adduce scientific evidence that it was such an attitude which caused the refusal to dehypnotise and not for some other reason. However, failure to dehypnotise as a result of the hypnotiser's aggressive attitude, where foresight is present, must technically be regarded as Cunningham recklessness.

Recklessness as a form of *mens rea* is only applicable: where a hypnotic trance is not properly and thoroughly terminated; when a hypnotiser makes no attempt to terminate the trance; and failure of the subject to dehypnotise due to the aggressive attitude of the hypnotist.

Negligence

As a form of *mens rea* negligence is quite rare in criminal law. This is not the case in civil law where a person is liable in the tort of negligence when there is a breach of a duty of care which is owed to another (see Chapter 13). In criminal law a person is negligent if his conduct falls below that of a reasonable man in the same circumstances. It will be perceived that negligence, as a form of *mens rea* is totally objective unlike the Cunningham subjective tests of recklessness.

Negligence features in only two common law offences of voluntary manslaughter and public nuisance, but it does arise in a limited number of statutory offences.

However, criminal assault, by virtue of the Criminal Justice Act 1988 and the Offences Against the Person Act 1861, does not feature in these statutory offences. Lord Ackner in the case of *R v Savage* [1992] stated:

"However, the history of the interpretation of the Act of 1861 shows that [...] the courts have consistently held that the mens rea of every type of offence against the person covers both actual intent and recklessness [...]"

Negligence, as a form of *mens rea* can therefore be eliminated as being a component of criminal assault.

The clear conclusion of the above examination of criminal assault and *mens rea* as an essential element of a crime, is that it is only applicable to recklessness. In addition, nontermination of a trance, in the three hypnotic circumstances above specified, is the only situation where recklessness is operative.

The above reference by Lord Ackner to 'the Act of 1861' is to the Offences Against the Person Act that contains the criminal assault offences in which this practice guide is interested.

Offences Against the Person Act 1861

There are two criminal assault offences by virtue of Section 39 of the Criminal Justice Act 1988. They are an 'assault' which makes the victims fear that unlawful force is about to be used against them and 'battery' which consists of the application of unlawful force where, for example, a mere touch can be sufficient. Under Section 39, there is no necessity to prove pain or harm. These offences are discounted as any injury arising would be very minor and transient and therefore not DSM-IV listed.

Three offences of criminal assault contained in the Offences Against the Person Act 1861 (OAP Act) are relevant.

Section 47

This section (as amended) of the OAP Act provides: 'Whosoever shall be convicted [...] of any assault occasioning actual bodily harm shall be liable to imprisonment for not more than five years'. This offence is commonly known as actual bodily harm (ABH) and to complete the offence physical injury must include 'hurt or injury calculated to interfere with health or comfort'. (*R v Miller* [1954]). Thus, ABH arises where mere discomfort is occasioned to the victim, but in *R v Chan-Fook* [1994] it was stated that injury 'should not be so trivial as to be wholly insignificant.' A good example of bodily harm under this section would be bruising.

In the case of Savage [1992] it was held that because unlawful force was intended there was no need to prove intention or recklessness, as forms of *mens rea*, in a case of ABH because they were already deemed to be present.

Section 20

This section (as amended) provides that: 'Whosoever shall unlawfully and maliciously inflict any grievous bodily harm upon any other person, with or without any weapon or instrument, [...] shall be liable to imprisonment for not more than five years'. This offence is generally known as 'unlawful wounding' requiring the breaking of the victim's skin, thereby causing bleeding, breaking bones or internal injury. The phrase 'grievous bodily harm' means really serious injury.

In relation to recklessness as a form of *mens rea*, 'maliciously' meant intentionally or recklessly (within the meaning of the Cunningham case). The wording of the Section 20 offence includes the word 'maliciously'.

Section 18

Finally, Section 18 (as amended) provides: 'Whosoever shall unlawfully and maliciously by any means whatsoever cause any grievous bodily harm to any person with intent to do some grievous bodily harm [...] shall be liable to imprisonment for life.'

This offence is similar to Section 20 unlawful wounding but, while recklessness as a form of *mens rea* is appropriate for Section 20, it is intention that is required for Section 18 offences, with it being specifically mentioned in the section. Life imprisonment is the maximum Section 18 sentence instead of five years imposed by both Section 47 and Section 20, with the reason for this much increased sentence being that greater moral fault is attributed to Section 18 offences.

The presence of *mens rea* as an essential element of a crime, must next be located in relation to the dangers of hypnosis where serious injury arises, with particular reference to the above trilogy of sections. The only such relevant danger to be considered is that of nontermination of a hypnotic trance in the three circumstances previously identified. Neither intent nor negligence, as forms of *mens rea*, are appropriate to nontermination of a hypnotic trance in the specified circumstances, but recklessness was certainly applicable.

Both Section 47 and Section 20 assaults accept recklessness as a form of *mens rea*. However, even though the word 'maliciously' – also meaning recklessly – appears in the Section 18 assault definition, such word is overridden because the offence is required to be committed 'with intent'. Offences under Section 18 are therefore discounted in this guide when considering psychological injury arising from any of the given reasons for non-termination of a hypnotic trance.

Bodily Harm

Is psychological injury able to form part of the 'bodily harm' mentioned in the three sections of the OAP Act?

Prior to 1997, there were a few High Court cases which admitted psychological (often alternatively referred to as 'psychiatric') harm to assault offences. In that year the Law Lords, in the combined appeal cases of *R v Burstow* and *R v Ireland* delivered judgements which eliminated any doubts which had previously existed. Furthermore, some related matters were included in the judgements that are of considerable assistance to this guide.

Delivering the leading judgement Lord Steyn notes that the issue of whether psychiatric illness is capable of amounting to bodily harm focuses on the law regarding *actus reus* and not *mens rea*. This guide has already restricted the applicability of injury arising from non-termination to Section 47 and Section 20 because of the law regarding *mens rea*.

Lord Steyn states, *inter alia*, in his judgement that:

> "The proposition that the Victorian legislator when enacting Sections 18, 20 and 47 of the Act (of) 1861, would not have had in mind psychiatric illness is no doubt correct. Psychiatry was in its infancy in 1861. But the subjective intention of the draftsman is immaterial. The only relevant enquiry is as to the sense of the words in the context in which they are used. Moreover the Act of 1861 is a statute of the "always speaking" type: the statute must be interpreted in the light of the best current scientific appreciation of the link between the body and psychiatric injury. […] I would hold that "bodily harm" in sections 18, 20 and 47 must be interpreted so as to include recognizable psychiatric illness."

As a result of this judgement it was held that 'recognisable psychiatric illness' was regarded as bodily harm. This means that such illness arising from the danger of non-termination of a hypnotic trance, in the circumstances earlier described, qualifies as bodily injury for the purposes of Section 47 and Section 20 of the OAP Act 1861.

One of the important and relevant matters featured in these appeal cases is that accused persons were liable even though there was no physical contact with the victims. For example, in the Ireland case, the victim was harassed over the telephone which the Telecommunications Act 1984 makes it an offence to cause annoyance, inconvenience or needless anxiety to another, There is, of course, no physical contact in hypnosis, including the nontermination of a trance.

Another matter in Lord Steyn's judgement is his reference to 'recognizable psychiatric illness'. DSM-IV was first introduced in Chapter 4 and has since been regularly and frequently referred to with the listed mental disorders (otherwise called illnesses) being set out in Part I of Appendix B (p. 191). These serious adverse effects (i.e. bodily harm) are reflected in Sections 47 and 20 of the OAP Act 1861 and being recognised psychiatric illnesses are listed in DSM-IV.

In his judgement, Lord Steyn also mentions anxiety neurosis and acute depression as examples of 'serious psychiatric illness'. Significantly these are disorders listed in DSM-IV and are also noted by McHovec (1986) and his medical colleagues as complications encountered by them in hypnotherapeutic practice (see

Part II of Appendix B (p. 193)). Lord Steyn distinguishes serious psychiatric illness from emotion such as fear. At the same time he also discounted transient and common every day complaints such as nausea, dizziness and headaches (see subheading 'Nature of psychological injury in assault' in Chapter 4).

When first introducing the three statutory assault sections earlier in this chapter they were expressed to be in ascending order of seriousness according to the injury inflicted. There is no guidance in the Burstow and Ireland appeal cases in respect of the allocation of psychiatric illnesses between the sections. The serious adverse effects arising from the non-termination of a hypnotic trance should belong to Section 20, because these adverse effects are far more serious and potentially longer lasting than those which would be admitted to Section 47.

Chapter 11
Civil Assault

Assault and Battery

Civil assault, as part of 'assault and battery' (otherwise known as 'trespass to the person') is similar to criminal assault contained in Section 39 of the Criminal Justice Act 1988 (see Chapter 10). It is merely an offer of force or violence by a person to another with the former being apparently capable of, and intending to commit an act of violence upon the latter, who believes he is actually threatened. This guide is not interested in this form of assault, but only in the 'battery' part of assault and battery, which is commonly, and in this guide, called assault.

Halisbury's Laws of England (1985, p. 602) defines the aforesaid battery as:

> A battery is an act of the defendant which directly and either intentionally or negligently causes some physical contact with the person of the plaintiff without the plaintiff's consent.

From the battery definition 'an act of the defendant' is the *actus reus* of an assault and this must be a 'physical' act with 'contact' being made with the victim. Usually an assault involves blows, with or without a weapon, stabbing, kicking and so on, but it does not have to include personal contact. It has been held that: the throwing of water over the plaintiff; pulling a chair away; taking fingerprints without permission; pulling something from the plaintiff's gasp; and applying a rinse to the hair, are all assaults. There is no necessity for the plaintiff to be of a hostile attitude, but, for example, a prank, or even an unwanted kiss, will suffice.

The plaintiff must prove that it was an unlawful act which, in accordance with the same definition, 'directly' caused the contact forming part of the assault. It is from this causation, being another aspect of the definition, that injury arises and a right of action is established.

The final aspect of the definition to be considered are the words 'either intentionally or negligently' which is the *mens rea* element of the assault. Unlike the most complicated mens rea in criminal law, the *mens rea* in civil assault is very straightforward.

Michael A. Jones, a Professor of Law at Liverpool University, describes intention in civil law as:

> Intention refers to the defendant's knowledge that the consequences of his conduct are bound to occur, where the consequences are desired or, if not desired, are foreseen as a certain result. (1998, p. 9.)

Intention in civil assault therefore closely follows the meaning in everyday life.

'Negligently' is linked to 'intentionally' as an alternative in the Halisbury's definition and simply means a careless act on the part of the defendant. This is where the difference lies between a right of action in trespass to the person and negligence lies. In *Fowler v Lanning* [1964], Lord Denning stated: "The only cause of action [...] where the injury was unintentional is negligence."

The Court of Appeal in *Wilson v Pringle* [1986] confirmed the Lord Denning directive and decided that where the contact is unintentional the plaintiff's claim for damages should be in the tort of negligence, but retains in the tort of assault any intentional acts by the defendant.

Chapter 13 examines the tort of negligence with particular reference to any liability which may accrue to the hypnotiser. Thus, the complete potential liability of the hypnotiser, at both criminal and civil law, are discussed in this book.

The 1985 definition of battery from Halisbury's Laws of England is deliberately used, not only for its comprehensiveness, but also to emphasise that, since the case of *Wilson v Pringle*, negligence as a form of *mens rea* is excluded from the tort of assault as a form of legal action.

There remains one important aspect of civil assault to be examined – psychological harm. The type of psychological (otherwise known as psychiatric) injury in which this guide is interested is contained within DSM-IV (see Part I of Appendix B (p. 191)).

It is well established in civil law that a defendant may be liable for psychological injury caused by his or her conduct. This injury in civil law is referred to as 'medically recognised psychiatric illness'. In *Alcock v Chief Constable of the South Yorkshire Police* [1991] it was stated that psychiatric damage comprised 'all relevant forms of mental illness, neurosis and personality change'. In the same case emotional stress, anguish and grief was distinguished as not being eligible for an award of damages.

Throughout this book DSM-IV has been adopted as the benchmark in separating serious psychological injury, as part of an illegal assault, from everyday minor and transient complaints. Using DSM-IV, which lists the 'medically recognised psychiatric illnesses', is again justified, but this time in civil assault.

Assault and Hypnosis

The mere fact that the *actus reus* of assault must be a physical act, and also contact must be made with the person (i.e. body) of the plaintiff, immediately disqualifies the induction of a hypnotic trance, and other associated procedures, from constituting a civil assault. This means that even in the event of DSM-IV listed injury being caused by the application of a therapy, or in the three circumstances of failure to dehypnotise (see Chapters 6 and 7 respectively) the tort of assault and battery is not available to an injured plaintiff in seeking damages.

Even if this were not the case, the lack of mens rea would defeat an action in assault. The only form of *mens rea* now recognised in assault is intent, which is certainly not present in the application of a hypnotic therapy. In this situation any consequential DSM-IV listed injuries are most certainly not 'bound to occur', or 'foreseen certain to result' by the hypnotiser, in accordance with the Jones definition set out earlier. It would also be the same situation with injury arising from the aforesaid failure to dehypnotise.

Therefore, whilst DSM-IV listed injuries are generally recognised in civil law as the type of psychological injuries upon which a plaintiff may rely in seeking damages, they are not applicable in the tort of assault in the above circumstances. However, this does not mean a psychologically injured plaintiff is not able to seek a remedy in another tort, such as in negligence. For example, even though the plaintiff failed in the case of *Gates v McKenna* [1998], because he had a pre-existing condition, his action for damages, in the absence of intent, was properly founded in negligence This case is again referred to in Chapter 13 when the relationship between the hypnotist and the tort of negligence is examined (see sub-subheading of 'Danger of precipitating a mental disorder', p. 154).

Even when DSM-IV listed injury arises from the application of a hypnotic therapy, or the three circumstances of the non-termination of a trance, the injured person has no right of action in the tort of assault.

Chapter 12

Consent

The matter of a person consenting to an illegal assault has been briefly mentioned in this book upon many occasions. In both criminal law and at civil law 'consent' concerns whether a person can agree to being the subject of an assault, with or without resultant injury, and also if such a consent negates any criminal offence, or liability as a tort-feasor. This chapter examines the law generally relating to consent as a defence to assault and in particular where there is a hypnosis involvement. In addition the meaning of 'informed consent' to a trespass to the person is explained and it is then considered whether this type of consent can be applied to illegal assault associated with hypnosis.

Consent and Criminal Assault

There are three elements of a crime, being *actus reus*, *mens rea* and the absence of a valid defence (see Chapter 10).

In the lawbreaking case of *R v Brown* and other appeals [1994] the Law Lords decided, whilst consent is a defence to common assault (that is, assault and battery contrary to Section 39 of the Criminal Justice Act 1988), it is no defence to an assault occasioning ABH, or to unlawful wounding (wounding). These two offences, contrary to Sections 47 and 20 of the Offences Against the Person Act 1861 (OAP Act), were discussed in Chapter 10, together with wounding with intent contrary to Section 18 of the same Act. However, there are some important exceptions to the law which not only allow minor assaults, but also the infliction of ABH and wounding where consent is impliedly, or expressly, granted by the injured party.

There is a considerable overlap between instances of consent as a defence at criminal law and in civil assault and, therefore, what appears immediately below applies to both, unless otherwise stated.

An assault technically occurs every time there is contact between humans, whether it is a congratulatory slap on the back, being jostled in a crowded shop, or merely shaking hands as an introduction. In these and many other situations the consent to the assault is implied, otherwise a person could accumulate dozens of actionable assaults each day. However, the implied consent is vitiated if, for example, someone in a crowded street is deliberately pushed over and suffers injury.

Likewise, in sports, such as rugby or football, the participants consent to contact with other players that arise within the rules of the game. However, a player does not consent to contact with another which would not be reasonably expected to be found within the game. Such contacts would be punching (except in boxing) and deliberate kicking of a player, with or without the ball. In these circumstances a offending player could be liable to criminal prosecution for assault under the OAP Act 1861 and, in addition, to a civil action for damages in respect of injury sustained. In the Court of Appeal case of *Condon v Basi* [1985] Sir John Donaldson, as Master of the Roll, stated of the defendant, who had broken the plaintiff's leg upon a late tackle, that "[...] He acted in a way to which the plaintiff cannot be expected to have consented". Therefore, a player assumes the risk of injury, but only that which could reasonably be expected depending on the nature of the sport.

Consent by the subject is to be found in the acts of tattooists and those persons who are engaged in body piercing. Referring to the case of *R v Brown* and other appeals [1994], several of their Lordships mentioned tattooing and confirmed it as being an activity to which a person could consent, whereby the offence of ABH was not committed. The reason is that it is not against public policy to acquire bodily decoration and adornment. It could perhaps be argued that consent is negated in the event of the tattooist creating the wrong tattoo, or not placing it in the position directed. The exception to the general rule, of persons not being able to consent to ABH and wounding upon themselves, would thereby cease to apply.

These are some of the general exceptions to the rule that a person cannot consent to acts of assaults being committed upon his or her person. However, this is subject to a specific exception in this chapter with regard to 'informed consent', where in certain circumstances a patient can validly consent to surgical treatment.

Once again referring to the House of Lords case of *R v Brown* and other appeals [1994] of which the facts were unlikely to be disputed as the defendants, belonging to a group of sado-masochistic homosexuals, recorded their activities by video camera. The group participated in acts of violence committed against each other, including upon the genital area, which engendered sexual pleasure by way of giving and receiving pain in both the aggressor and victim. The defendants were charged with offences under both Section 47 and Section 20 of the OAP Act 1861 on the basis, according to the prosecution, that the so-called victims could not consent to the assaults being carried out on themselves. The Law Lords agreed with the prosecution and the appellants' convictions for ABH and wounding were confirmed.

In his judgement, Lord Templeman observed:

> "In principle there is a difference between violence which is incidental and violence which is inflicted for the indulgence of cruelty. The violence of sado-masochistic encounters involves the indulgence of cruelty by sadists and the degradation of victims. I am not prepared to invent a defence of consent for sado-masochistic encounters which breed and glorify cruelty and result in offences under Sections 47 and 20 of the Act of 1861."

In the same judgement, Lord Templeman compares the activities in the *Brown* case to surgery and other lawful activities by stating:

> "Other activities carried on with consent by or on behalf of the injured person have been accepted as lawful notwithstanding that they involve actual bodily harm or may cause serious bodily harm. Ritual circumcision, tattooing, ear-piercing and violent sports, including boxing are lawful activities ... "

Lord Templeman appears to establish a dividing line between consensual behaviour which does not constitute criminal assault (i.e. the exceptions to the general rule) and unlawful behaviour to which a person cannot consent. However, this dividing line is not entirely clear which is illustrated by the case of *R v Wilson* [1996]. The facts were that the defendant was convicted of assault (ABH) having used a hot knife to brand his initials on his wife's buttocks, with her complete consent and, indeed, at her instigation. Wilson's appeal to the Court of Appeal was allowed partly on the basis that it would not be in the public interest that such activity of the defendant should be treated as criminal behaviour, particularly as it '[...] was [not] any more dangerous or painful than tattooing'.

In the same case, Lord Justice Russell stated:

> "Consensual activity between husband and wife, in the privacy of the matrimonial home, is not, in our judgement, a proper matter for criminal investigation, let alone criminal prosecution. In this field, in our judgement, the law should develop upon a case by case basis rather than upon general propositions to which, in the changing times we live, exceptions may arise from time to time not expressly covered by authority."

One of the 'general propositions' impliedly referred to by Lord Justice Russell is, no doubt, the above cited case of Brown, which is specifically quoted elsewhere in the Wilson judgement. It seems likely that the court did not place Wilson's behaviour in the same moral category as the defendants in the Brown case and therefore used the excuse of relating it to tattooing. As a result the court created another exception to the general rule of not being able to consent to either ABH or wounding offences where similar and consensual behaviour to that in Wilson, is in private between husband and wife.

Criminal Assault, Hypnosis and Consent

The only criminal responsibility to arise out of the induction of a hypnotic trance, and related procedures, were three circumstances of failure to terminate a trance. These three circumstances – to be found in all three major hypnotic settings – are: failure of the hypnotiser to properly and thoroughly terminate the trance; the hypnotiser making no attempt whatsoever to terminate; and the subject refusing to dehypnotise due to the aggressive attitude of the hypnotiser. However, the last circumstance is discounted for the reason set out in Chapter 10 (see sub-subheading on 'Recklessness') and only the other two circumstances of nontermination are considered in connection with consent, as a defence to criminal assault. The two circumstances of nontermination, which can arise in all three major settings, means the element of consent has to be considered in each of them.

In the laboratory the consent of the subject (often college students who are usually paid a fee, or receive a course credit) must be implied when he or she volunteers to be involved in hypnosis research and experimentation.

Next, it could be argued that a client upon making an appointment with a hypnotherapist is implying consent to be hypnotised upon their subsequent meeting for therapeutic reasons. In any event keeping the appointment with the hypnotherapist is certainly implied consent in a clinical setting.

Finally, to be considered is consent in a stage setting for entertainment purposes. In the previously cited case of *Gates v McKenna* [1998] the defendant maintained that by taking part in the show, Gates had consented to participating in a series of silly sketches. The implied consent to being hypnotised must be when the subject volunteers to go on the stage. The implied consent in each of the above three major settings could be granted in writing (highly unlikely in the stage setting), but such express written consent would have no different effect to implied consent. Express or implied consents must not be confused with informed consent.

There can be no doubt that a valid consent to the induction of a hypnotic trance, together with allied procedures, is present in each of the three major settings in the above circumstances. However, consent must be restricted to the agreed purpose for which a hypnotic trance was induced, with the consent becoming inoperative if the hypnotist goes off on a frolic of his own. For example, in Chapter 8 there are mentioned a number of studies that relate how a hypnotherapist allegedly coerced a female client into having sexual intercourse, to which she had not consented.

Furthermore, the implied consents in the three major settings cannot extend to the criminal infliction of bodily harm by way of adverse psychological effects of the nature listed in DSM-IV. This is abundantly clear from the above cited case of *R v Brown* and other appeals [1994] which debars serious acts of assault (i.e. contrary to Section 47 and Section 20 of the OAP Act 1861) from being the subject of consent and thereby prevents a person, who inflicts bodily harm, escaping criminal prosecution.

Despite the presence of consent this means that where DSM-IV listed injury arises upon a hypnotiser not properly and thoroughly terminating a hypnotic trance, or not making any effort to termi-nate, such hypnotiser is liable for prosecution for ABH or wounding.

The ever influential Law Commission, published Consultation Paper No. 139 in 1995 entitled 'Consent in the Criminal Law'. The Commission proposed, among other things, that:

> [...] The reckless causing of seriously disabling injury should continue to be criminal, even if the injured person consents to such injury or the risk of such injury. (Para. 4.48(1).)

Recklessness as a form of *mens rea* in criminal law is compatible with both the assaults of ABH and wounding, which can arise by virtue of nontermination.

The above Law Commission proposal, together with many others in the same paper, is not yet contained in a statute, but it does demonstrate the manner in which high ranking lawyers and others are thinking about the law relating to consent. It is, of course, in accordance with the decision in Brown with regard to a victim not being able to consent to the infliction of bodily harm (which expression includes DSM-IV listed illnesses), subject only to the established exceptions discussed earlier in this chapter.

Interestingly, the Commission in the same paper included in its definition of 'seriously disabling injury' the '[...] Serious impair-ment of mental health [...]' (para. 4.51(2)). This reference to injury could easily be interpreted as the psychological adverse conditions listed in DSM-IV.

However, despite the decision in *R v Brown* and other appeals [1994] and the Law Commission proposal on recklessness and con-sent, this guide must consider if the courts might create a new exception. This proposed new exception would consider allowing consent as a defence to criminal acts of bodily harm arising from hypnosis. It would, of course, apply to the two circumstances of nontermination, with it being considered in a clinical setting only.

There are a number of factors in support of such a new exception which arose in both Brown and the later case of *R v Wilson* [1996]. Lord Templeman in Brown is quoted above as differentiating between bodily harm which is incidental to the main purpose of the consensual behaviour and bodily harm arising from 'violence which is inflicted for the indulgence of cruelty'. In a clinical setting the consensual behaviour (i.e. to the induction of a hypnotic trance and other allied procedures) is for the purpose of the betterment of the client's health and any injury arising from non-termination would be incidental.

Furthermore, in his judgement Lord Templeman refers to lawful activities (e.g. tattooing) to which a victim may properly consent even though resulting in bodily harm. Hypnotherapy is certainly a lawful activity from which bodily harm may emanate from the nontermination of a hypnotic trance in the two circumstances mentioned earlier.

Another factor, in support of hypnotherapy becoming an exception to the general rule of consent as a defence, is one of the reasons given by the Court of Appeal in Wilson. Such reason was that the activity of the defendant, in branding his wife's buttocks in private, was not in the public interest to be treated as criminal behaviour. Admittedly the relationship between hypnotherapist and client is not as close as husband and wife, but the bodily harm arises from what one could a 'special relationship', of which some would regard as akin to that of doctor and patient. In addition the hypnotherapeutic activity is carried out in a private place.

In final support, of the prospect of hypnotherapy perhaps becoming an exception in due course, are the words of Lord Justice Russell from the Wilson case which are set out above, and refer to the law being developed upon 'a case by case basis', because 'exceptions may arise from time to time'.

Upon the above bases it would initially appear that consent in hypnosis could be a good candidate to become an exception to the general rule that a person cannot consent to the infliction of bodily harm upon himself, or herself, contrary to sections 47 and 20 of the OAP Act 1861. Both these sections require intent or recklessness as forms of *mens rea*. It was intent that was present in both *Brown and other appeals* [1994] and *R v Wilson* [1996], but it is recklessness which causes the non-termination of a hypnotic trance from which DSM-IV type injury may arise.

The point is that in both the Brown and Wilson cases the defendants, and their victims, were aware that pain and suffering was to be inflicted and also its approximate extent. Furthermore, the consenting wife in Wilson knew that there would be residual disfigurement on her buttocks (regarded by her as decoration in similar manner to tattooing) and again could imagine the extent of the bodily harm. However, this foresight would not be present in the reckless nontermination of a hypnotic trance, because the victim upon granting consent to being subjected to hypnotic procedures, would not perceive the infliction, or extent of bodily harm which could arise.

It is understandable that consent was valid as a defence in the Wilson case, to what otherwise would be criminal activity. As a result this case – involving intent as a form of *mens rea* is an exception to the general rule of a person being unable to consent to the infliction of serious bodily harm (which expression includes DSM-IV listed adverse conditions) – on another. However, where recklessness is involved (e.g. failure by a hypnotiser to terminate a trance) it is undeniably sensible of the law to exclude consent as a defence to an activity resulting in ABH and wounding. The basis of this statement is that a person cannot properly consent to being subjected to injury of which he or she is unaware and, in any event, is unable to quantify.

Civil Assault, Hypnosis and Consent

It was decided in Chapter 11 that the induction of a hypnotic trance and other connected procedures did not constitute a civil assault, even if DSM-IV listed injuries were caused. It was stated that a person suffering from DSM-IV listed psychological harm may have a valid claim in the tort of negligence, but certainly not in assault, arising from non-termination of a trance in the two circumstances identified earlier.

There is one further aspect of consent which has not yet been considered and that is 'informed consent' to which one wonders whether it can be applied to hypnosis.

Informed Consent

A basic principle of medical care in the United Kingdom is that, with certain exceptions such as minors, a person has an absolute right at common law (countrywide rules of law – as opposed to local customs – developed in the three centuries after the Norman Conquest in 1066) to grant or withhold consent to treatment.

Most of the time consent is implied, for example, when a patient submits to a physical examination, or offers an arm for the purpose of giving blood. In such circumstances there is no necessity for the doctor, or other health professional, to seek express (oral or written) consent. However, it is a different matter in those situations where 'informed consent' is most important to protect medical personnel.

The Oxford Concise Medical Dictionary of 1998 defines 'informed consent' as:

> A legal requirement that physicians or researchers inform a patient undergoing surgery or invasive tests or a subject involved in a clinical trial of the nature, risks and probable outcome of the treatment or research. (p. 334)

This type of consent is another exception to the general rule that a person cannot consent to serious injury being inflicted upon himself or herself.

Informed consent, as a form of defence, applies to assault at both criminal and civil law and as a result exculpates a doctor from criminal prosecution and liability for damages in the tort of trespass to the person – again alternatively called 'assault'. (The word 'doctor' is a description used in this chapter to include all medically qualified persons – including clinical researchers – who perform surgery or invasive procedures.) This does not mean a doctor can always hide behind an informed consent. In *Sidaway v Bethlem Royal Hospital Governors* [1985] it was stated:

> It is only if the consent is obtained by fraud or by misrepresentation of the true nature of what is to be done that it can be said that an apparent consent is not a true consent. This is the position in the criminal law [...] and the cause of action based on trespass to the person is closely analogous.

As a result fraud or misrepresentation will invalidate a patient's consent to surgery.

Informed consent is subject to a doctor informing the patient of the 'nature, risks and probable outcome' of surgery (a description deemed to include invasive tests). By this means the consent becomes informed. Whilst there is no necessity for a doctor to obtain informed consent in writing, it is prudent to do so, because there can then be no doubt of the terms. All NHS hospitals use written forms of consent with the Department of Health dictating the format.

It is eminently sensible of the law to allow surgery to be carried out without the doctor, and the hospital vicariously, being liable in the tort of assault provided, of course, a proper informed consent is first obtained. This is irrespective of a successful outcome of the surgery, but even in that event without an informed consent – though actionable *per se* (i.e. without proof of damage) – it is likely only nominal damages would be awarded and a plaintiff could be penalised in costs.

It is important to bear in mind that where the offending behaviour is intentional, informed consent is a defence to trespass to the person, but not where the behaviour is unintentional when the plaintiff's claim is in negligence (see Chapter 13 for a full discussion upon the law of negligence with particular reference to the hypnotist). One is thereby reminded of the earlier cited case of *Wilson v Pringle* [1986] (see subheading of 'Assault and battery' in Chapter 11) by way of a plaintiff claiming in either assault or negligence.

Generally, a person cannot exclude liability in respect of his or her own negligence, with the exclusion not being able to form part of an informed consent, which is restricted to considerations of assault only. This distinction features in the later discussion relating to the above mentioned nature, risks and probable outcome of surgery carried out by a doctor.

The three integral elements at the heart of informed consent, being the nature, risks and probable outcome, are now examined. Underlying these elements is the sufficiency of information given to the patient to enable an informed decision to be made whether or not to go ahead with the proposed surgery.

To understand the nature of the proposed surgery the patient must be informed of the procedure to which he or she is being asked to consent. This does not mean that the nature of the surgery has to be described in detail, step by step. In *Chatterton v Gerson* [1981] it was held that a consent was valid once the nature of the intended procedure had been explained in 'broad terms'. In this case the plaintiff suffered partial immobility of a leg, due to numbness caused by a second injection with a different type of drug injected close to the spinal cord, about which the surgeon had not informed her before the operation. The court decided that the plaintiff was under no illusion as to the general nature of the proposed procedure and therefore her consent was valid. This was an important decision for doctors who, whilst acting in good faith, were held not to be liable for an intentional act in the tort of trespass to the person, provided a proper informed consent – on the lines of the Chatterton case – had been earlier obtained.

The Chatterton decision does not exclude any liability in negligence where the defendant doctor can be liable for lack of information regarding the risks associated with a particular procedure. The exclusion of one's own liability in negligence is mentioned earlier. This means that whilst 'risks' are properly included in the above quoted definition of informed consent, the courts distinguish between lack of information regarding the nature of the procedure and its risks. Thus, a doctor not providing any information whatsoever in respect of the nature of a surgical procedure would be liable to the patient in assault, whereas a doctor, even with consent, could be liable in negligence if there was lack of information about any risks which resulted in injury.

In the definition of informed consent the 'probable outcome of the treatment' essentially refers to a prognosis of the patient's health after the treatment. Any lack of information would be treated in similar manner to that of 'risks' above in that it would be negligent of a doctor not to provide a full and accurate prognosis.

From such a prognosis and information concerning the nature of the procedure, together with the associated risks, the patient should be in a position to make a balanced judgement to proceed with the surgery and, in that event, properly grant informed consent.

Informed consent and hypnosis

The only liability in assault, arising from all the dangers of hypnosis, is that relating to non-termination where the trance is not thoroughly and properly terminated, or where the hypnotiser makes no attempt to terminate. The liability is at criminal law only, being contrary to Sections 47 and 20 of the Offences Against the Person Act 1861 (see Chapter 10). The above analysis of informed consent has revealed many reasons why it cannot apply to hypnosis and as a result not provide a defence to criminal assault arising from the non-termination of a hypnotic trance.

The primary reason why informed consent is not applicable to the induction of a hypnotic trance, and associated procedures, is that such consent is restricted to doctors who are proposing surgery, or invasive tests. This is, of course, far removed from the intended hypnotic influence upon the psyche.

Another good reason is that whilst the consent is concerned with assault arising from an intentional act by the doctor, the two circumstances of nontermination of a hypnotic trance arise from a reckless act by the hypnotiser.

One of the three integral elements of informed consent is the requirement that the nature of the procedure is explained to the patient, even though in broad terms. In Chapter 3, the main characteristics of hypnosis were readily described, but the nature was revealed to be in dispute even amongst the so-called experts. The dispute concerns the lack of consensus upon whether hypnosis is an altered state of consciousness, which has been the subject of the State v Nonstate ongoing debate for many years past. The point is, that because of this lack of consensus, a hypnotiser could not supply the required information in respect of the nature of the procedure (i.e. the induction of a hypnotic trance and allied procedures) in informed consent. A valid informed consent could not therefore be granted and provide a hypnotiser with a defence to criminal assault, in the two circumstances of nontermination referred to earlier.

Chapter 13

Negligence

Only serious psychological adverse effects arising in criminal and civil assault have been dealt with so far. To omit the tort of negligence, and associated psychological injury would leave the legal liability of a hypnotiser incomplete. This chapter covers the complete liability of a hypnotiser at English law, with regard to psychological injury. It should be added that negligence rarely features in a crime, with it being largely confined to driving offences and the serious offence of manslaughter.

Martin's (1995, p. 263) simple definition of civil negligence informs us that it is, 'A tort consisting of the breach of a duty of care resulting in damage to the plaintiff.' There are three interrelated elements in this definition. First, a duty of care, next, a breach of that duty of care and, last, damage to the plaintiff resulting from the breach of the duty of care. These three elements are so closely related it sometimes means they overlap.

Duty of Care

Ask any lawyer what he or she considers to be the most important and well known case in civil law the answer will invariably be the 1932 case of *Donoghue v Stevenson*. This case concerned a bottle of ginger beer containing a decomposed snail which made the consumer ill. The manufacturers were held to be in breach of a duty of care owed to the consumer even though no contractual relationship existed between them.

In the *Donoghue v Stevenson* case, Lord Atkin in his judgement, referring to the principle of a duty of care, stated:

> The rule that you are to love your neighbour becomes in law, you must not injure your neighbour; and the lawyer's question, Who is my neighbour? receives a restricted reply. You must take reasonable care to avoid acts and omissions which you held can reasonably foresee would be likely to injure

your neighbour. Who, then, in law is my neighbour? The answer seems to be – persons who are so closely and directly affected by my act that I ought reasonably to have them in contemplation as being so affected when I am directing my mind to the acts or omissions which are called in question.

The principle of a duty of care is based upon the concept of reasonable foresight and it is this concept upon which the criterion of negligence was established by *Donohue v Stevenson* and continues today.

However, *Donoghue v Stevenson* is not restricted to those cases which involve a manufacturer's duty to a consumer, because its applicability has been extended ever since. Lord Reid emphasised this point in *Dorset Yacht Co. v Home Office* when he said:

> [...] There has been a steady trend towards regarding the law of negligence as depending on principle so that, when a new point emerges, one should ask not whether it is covered by authority but whether recognised principles apply to it. *Donoghue v. Stevenson* may be regarded as a milestone, and the well-known passage in Lord Atkin's speech should I think be regarded as a statement of principle. It is not to be treated as if it were a statutory definition. It will require qualification in new circumstances. But I think that the time has come when we can and should say it ought to apply unless there is some justification or valid explanation for its exclusion.

A most important part of this quotation is the last sentence which states that the principle of the duty of care, established in *Donoghue v Stevenson*, is one of general application unless there are clear reasons to the contrary.

The concept of reasonable foresight (or foreseeability), is central to the question of the duty of care in negligence cases and therefore demands closer examination.

Jones (1998, p. 32) states that the concept of foreseeability is '[...] what a "reasonable man" would have foreseen in the circumstances [...]'. There are serious difficulties in applying this concept of reasonable foresight to a set of circumstances as foreseen by a hypothetical 'reasonable man'. Given a set of circumstances, where the range of an occurrence is from near certainty to almost impossible, any two so-called reasonable men could easily disagree upon the forseeability. This situation is not helped by the courts who have regarded defendants liable for loss where the range was from reasonably foreseeable as a possibility to very likely. So much for the concept of foreseeability and the reasonable man. Taking into account these factors it is fair comment to state that the boundaries of reasonable foresight are flexible, to say the least.

However, the application of the reasonable man test in the context of foreseeability is not always appropriate. In an action for negligence, where the defendant holds himself, or herself, out as possessing a particular skill, the standard of care and skill must be at the same level as others exercising that skill in the same profession or calling. In these circumstances the test of the reasonable man is not applied. In the well-known High Court case of *Bolam v Friern Hospital Management Committee* it was decided:

> Where you get a situation which involves the use of some special skill or competence, then the test as to whether there has been negligence or not is not the test of the man on the top of a Clapham omnibus, because he has not got this special skill. The test is the standard of the ordinary skilled man exercising and professing to have that special skill [...]

The man on the top of the Clapham omnibus is, of course, the previously mentioned reasonable man, sometimes alternatively referred to as Mr Average.

This means that at first sight a defendant will be liable in negligence if he, or she, holds him or herself out as possessing a particular skill if there is a failure to exercise due care and skill, or if it was not possessed in the first place.

Even though the Bolam case was one based on medical negligence it must not be thought that it restricts the class of defendants to members of the medical profession. Percy (1990, p. 561), agreeing with many other writers and legal experts, advises, 'This duty to use reasonable care and skill is applicable generally to everyone, practising a calling involving personal skill.'

This special standard of skill has been held by the courts to apply to a huge range of practitioners (as well as medical personnel) including: accountants, solicitors, estate agents, engineers, dentists, company case directors, insurance brokers and valuers. This is an important aspect of the duty of care when considering the liability of hypnotisers.

Duty of care and the hypnotist

There are a number reasons why a duty of care is to be found between a hypnotiser and the subject. The reasons are reflected in the Lord Akin quotation from *Donoghue v Stevenson*. Lord Atkin, first of all, establishes the concept of reasonable foresight when stating that one must not 'injure your neighbour'. He then asks the question, 'Who then, in law, is my neighbour?' In answering this question he says, in terms, that 'my neighbour' is the person who should reasonably be in the defendant's mind as being affected by acts and omissions upon the part of such defendant.

Applying the Lord Atkin view to a hypnotic setting, one can clearly see that the neighbour is the subject and the other party is the hypnotist. The principle of the duty of care is applicable to any of the hypnotic settings in accordance with the earlier cited case of *Dorset Yacht Co. v Home Office*. It was established in this case that the principle is one of general application – provided there is no good reason to the contrary.

Therefore, the duty arises because the relationship imposes upon the hypnotist an obligation to take reasonable care for the benefit of the subject, with that duty of care existing in all three major settings, being hypnosis research and experimentation, clinical and upon the stage.

When applying the concept of foreseeability to the hypnotic context the question of whether a reasonable man should have foreseen the consequences is at the heart of the hypnotiser and subject relationship. Whatever the difficulties may be in applying this concept of foreseeability, no reasonable man could deny that a duty of care must exist, because a reasonable man would foresee injury, arising from the hypnotist and subject relationship, as being within Lord Atkin's 'neighbour' principle.

It follows that the hypnotiser's duty is to take reasonable care upon the induction of a hypnotic trance and also when other hypnotic procedures are applied. It may not, however, be the reasonable man test which is appropriate when considering reasonable foresight as part of the duty of care by a hypnotiser. Earlier in this chapter the matter of someone being held out as possessing a particular skill was considered. In that event it was stated it could be that the test is not that of a reasonable man, but that of others possessing and exercising a particular skill.

There is no case law to assist in deciding which approach to adopt whether it be the test is that of a reasonable man, or of persons skilled in the art of hypnosis. The hypnotiser is not to be found in the list of skilled people set out earlier where it was held by the courts that a duty of care existed. In the only reported court case involving hypnosis and psychological damage (see *Gates v McKenna* in Chapter 4 'Danger of precipitating a mental disorder'), where the plaintiff sued in the tort of negligence, the question of the foreseeability approach (i.e. a reasonable man or a special standard of care) was not specifically mentioned. However, throughout the case report it is abundantly clear that the notion of a special standard of care was implicit.

Breach of Duty of Care

The second element of the tort of negligence is a breach of the duty of care having, first of all, established that a duty of care exists. The reader may wish to regard a breach of the duty of care as an act of carelessness on the part of the defendant, which is a somewhat over simplistic, but still an accurate general description of a breach.

It is a two-stage process to ascertain if a person is in breach of a duty of care. The first of the two stages concerns the standard of care that a defendant should have reasonably achieved. Here, in common with establishing a duty of care examined above, the question of reasonable foreseeability is to be determined by the hypothetical 'reasonable man', or by persons who are skilled in the art of whatever activity they are engaged.

The second stage in the process of deciding if there is a breach in the duty of care is for the plaintiff to demonstrate that the defendant's conduct fell below an appropriate standard, taking into account all the circumstances of the case.

On the matter of whether damage to the plaintiff is a foreseeable consequence of the defendant's conduct it does not necessarily mean that a defendant is liable in negligence even if the damage was foreseeable. A good example is to be found in the House of Lords case of *Bolton v Stone*, which involved the plaintiff being injured by a cricket ball driven out of the ground into a quiet road. It was rare for a ball to be hit outside the ground and, in fact, it had only happened six times in 30 years. The court held that there was no liability attaching to the defendant because, in the circumstances, it was reasonable to ignore such a small risk. In the same case Lord Oaksey stated that a reasonable man can:

> [...] Foresee the possibility of many risks, but life would be almost impossible if he were to attempt to take precautions against every risk which he can foresee. He takes precautions against risks which are reasonably likely to happen.

It follows that for a defendant not to be liable in negligence, where the risk is foreseeable, there must be an examination of the degree of risk and also whether a standard of care can be reasonably expected in view of the magnitude of the risk. In the *Bolton v Stone* case where the risk was foreseeable, but the chance of it happening was very small, the court held that even though precautions could have been taken (such as erecting higher fences around the ground) it was not necessary to guard against such a small risk. Therefore, in the circumstances it was reasonable to ignore the risk. Lord Reid added:

> In the crowded conditions of modern life even the most careful person cannot avoid creating some risks and accepting others. What a man must not do is to create a risk which is substantial.

It must not, however, be thought that it is reasonable to ignore all foreseeable risks which are unlikely to happen. In these cases of the risk being small there must also be taken into account the circumstance of the practicability, or cost of taking precautions. If the high cost of taking precautions, such as the erection of fencing in the *Bolton v Stone* case, is vastly disproportionate to the small risk of harm to others, the court may hold that the risk was justified. As a result the courts where there is a foreseeable, even though small risk, will not necessarily insist upon the taking of precautions producing absolute safety if the cost of providing it is astronomical. On the other hand if the risk can be eliminated, if not substantially reduced by small, or no expenditure, the defendant would have acted unreasonably if he failed to do so.

This situation was recognised in *Overseas Tankship (UK) Ltd v Miller Steamship Co.* where the risk of spilled oil on sea water catching fire was foreseeable, but extremely small, and only required the closing of a valve to stop the discharge. The court stated that a reasonable man would not have ignored the small risk involved because, '[...] action to eliminate it presented no difficulty, involved no disadvantage and required no expense'.

So far, in considering a breach of duty of care, the standard of care is that assessed by a reasonable man, but, in similar fashion when discussing earlier whether a duty of care exists, the standard of a person professing a special skill is judged by others who possess such skill.

In this further circumstance to be taken into account the case of *Bolam v Friern Hospital Management Committee* is considered again. Mr Justice McNair stated:

> The test is the standard of the ordinary skilled man exercising and professing to have that particular skill. A man need not possess the highest expert skill at the risk of being found negligent [...] it is sufficient if he exercises the ordinary skill of an ordinary competent man exercising that particular art.

The court went on to find that negligence, '[...] means failure to act in accordance with the standards of reasonably competent medical men at the time'. While this case concerned the medical negligence of doctors the test referred to by McNair is not restricted to the medical profession, but is of general application as Percy (1990, 561) advised earlier. It has similarly also been held in *Gold v Haringey Health Authority* and other cases.

In practice a defendant wishing to rebut an allegation of negligence must adduce evidence, by way of witnesses in the same profession or calling, that he behaved in a manner which conformed to the standards of a reasonably competent person exercising and professing to have a particular skill.

However, where a defendant has carried out a task which ordinarily requires a particular skill, which he does not possess, he will still be judged by the objective standards of a reasonably competent man exercising that skill, but not in this circumstance by the hypothetical reasonable man. To illustrate this point one can look to the case of *Wells v Cooper* where the defendant was held responsible to the plaintiff for injuries caused to him as a result of the defendant negligently carrying out carpentry work on his house. The court was not saying that the defendant should have reached the standards of a professional carpenter executing the work for reward, but it should have been carried out by a person reasonably competent in the art of carpentry. However, it would have been a different matter if the defendant had explicitly held himself out as a professional carpenter, or professing to have the skill, whereupon he would have been expected to achieve an even higher standard.

Breach of duty and the hypnotist

One must look back at the dangers of hypnosis (see Chapters 6 to 9) to find if any breaches of the duty of care could arise because it is from the risk that damage to the subject may occur. In this context damage means adverse psychological effects which are discussed in greater detail later (see sub-subheading of 'Damage and the hypnotist', p. 44).

Serious adverse psychological effects, from acts or omissions on the part of the hypnotiser, can arise upon the non-termination of the hypnotic trance (see Chapter 7), either by the hypnotiser not properly and thoroughly terminating the trance, or making no attempt whatsoever to terminate. Such adverse effects can also arise upon the trance not terminating because the subject refuses to return to the fully conscious waking state as a result of the hypnotiser's aggressive attitude. However, in common with criminal assault, the refusal of the subject to return to the fully conscious state is also ignored, because of the practical difficulties in proving the connection between the refusal and the hypnotiser's aggressive attitude. It will be appreciated that the non-termination of a trance applies to all three major settings and in addition it applies to the amateur context which is separately mentioned later.

Other than nontermination of a hypnotic trance the only other instance of serious adverse psychological effects arising in hypnosis is surprisingly upon the application of therapies (see Chapter 6).

In assessing whether a hypnotiser is in breach of a duty of care, where serious adverse psychological effects arise upon nontermination of a hypnotic trance, one must initially decide the standard of care that the operator should have reasonably exercised. Thereafter, it must be demonstrated that the hypnotiser's conduct fell below that predetermined reasonable standard of care, in similar fashion to that in every other case of alleged negligence.

There can be no doubt that in all three major settings a hypnotiser will have not only been taught how to induce a hypnotic trance, but also how to terminate it. At the same time it is highly likely that the importance of a proper and thorough termination would have been emphasised or, at the least, mentioned and accompanied by warnings of the dangers in failing to do so. Even if a defending hypnotist were to deny any knowledge of serious adverse effects arising from nontermination he would still be adjudged not to have adopted a reasonable standard of care. The reason is that both a reasonable man, and more particularly hypnotist's peers, would say that the risk of adverse effects must be a foreseeable consequence of the failure to terminate the trance. The so-called reasonable man would no doubt decide there was a breach of the duty of care upon the logical basis that if a hypnotist knew how to induce a hypnotic trance in the first place he must have learned the procedure to terminate at the same time and warned of the perils upon failure to do so. Experts would, of course, know that psychological damage can arise as a foreseeable consequence of the non-termination of a hypnotic trance.

Obviously, there is a risk, but is it of a sufficient magnitude to constitute a breach of a reasonable standard of care, upon such a breach causing serious psychological adverse effects?

In the case of *Bolton v Stone*, Lord Reid stated: 'What a man must not do is to create a risk which is substantial.' While it cannot be said, with any degree of certainty, that the nontermination by the defendant creates a 'substantial' risk of injury to the subject, one must also take into account the words of Lord Oaksey, again in

Bolton v Stone: 'He takes precautions against risks which are reasonably likely to happen.'

This circumstance of taking precautionary measures is an important feature when considering a breach of a reasonable standard of care in hypnosis.

The cost of taking precautionary measures by the erection of fencing in *Bolton v Stone* was disproportionate to the small risk of injury to persons in the adjoining roads outside the cricket ground. In this case it was held that even though the risk of hitting a cricket ball out of the ground was foreseeable the degree of risk was very small (it had happened six times in 30 years) and it was therefore reasonable to ignore that risk. Furthermore, it was decided that no precautions – such as erecting fencing – need to have been taken to guard against the risk. Here the court took into account the high cost of providing absolute safety.

The precaution to be taken to avoid the risk of serious psychological injury in the present context would be a proper and thorough termination of the hypnotic trance by the hypnotiser. The financial cost of terminating a hypnotic trance is, of course, nil and thereby supports the view that a hypnotiser acts unreasonably if the trance is not properly and thoroughly terminated. Absolutely applicable to this aspect of the hypnotic context is the case of *Overseas Tankship (UK) Ltd v Miller Steamship Co.*, when it was stated that even a small risk must not be ignored where it could be eliminated without any difficulty and '[...] Involved no disadvantage and required no expense'.

Therefore, whether the risk created by a hypnotist upon failure to dehypnotise is Lord Reid's 'substantial', or small enough to ignore, it means that a hypnotist is in breach of a reasonable standard of a duty of care because the risk can be eliminated by taking precautionary measures at no financial cost. This must particularly be the case, in all three major settings, where hypnotists hold themselves out as possessing a special skill. Here the question of whether a duty of care exists, and if the operator is in breach of such a duty, is judged by '[...] An ordinary competent man exercising that particular art.' Thus, for example, in accordance with the Bolam case, the test applicable to whether a clinical hypnotherapist had achieved a reasonable standard of a duty of care would be the standard usually achieved by other ordinary competent hypnotherapists, who hold themselves out as possessing skills in the art of therapeutic hypnosis.

The status of a hypnotiser in the amateur context must also be considered. One can look to the above discussed case of Wells Cooper to determine the liability of a hypnotiser in this context which is normally confined to students who hope, for example, to cure another's exam nerves, or who are having fun at a party.

The *Wells v Cooper* case applied to amateur hypnotists means that they will be judged by the objective standards of a reasonably competent hypnotist who exercises the skill of a hypnotist in any of the other three major settings. This does not mean a court would expect the amateur hypnotist to achieve the standards of a professional hypnotiser (e.g. a full time practising hypnotherapist), but by a person reasonably competent in the art of hypnosis. If, however, the amateur had expressly held himself out as a professional hypnotist, or professed to have the skills, he would be expected to achieve an even higher standard than a reasonably competent hypnotist.

This is a principle which would also equally apply to any person holding himself out as a professional whether in an amateur setting, or any one of the other three major settings.

The tort of negligence was earlier referred to as simply an act of 'carelessness', but whether this description is suitable in respect of the other danger of hypnosis where serious adverse psychological effects may arise, has yet to be examined. This other danger arises upon the application of hypnotic therapies with the reasons discussed in Chapter 6 – 'Hypnosis in a clinical setting'.

The law of negligence applied to a breach of a duty of care in the case of the nontermination of a hypnotic trance is identical to that of serious adverse psychological effects arising upon the application of hypnotic therapies. Therefore, it is necessary to examine whether the hypnotiser should have reasonably foreseen a risk of injury to the subject, the degree of that risk and if such risk could be reduced, or even eliminated.

Unlike trainee hypnotisers being warned of the dangers of non-termination of a hypnotic trance the dangers arising from the application of therapies are highly unlikely to be mentioned at all. The reason is that serious adverse psychological effects arising from the clinical setting are relatively unknown. It is most surprising that hypnosis *per se* is not responsible for, nor associated with, serious adverse psychological effects. It is the therapeutic use of hypnosis which causes the ill effects.

Reasons proposed in respect of adverse effects arising from the application of therapies are set out in Chapter 6 – 'Hypnosis in a Clinical Setting'. One such proposed reason is that a hypnotic subject perceives the therapy as a threat and it is that threat which is responsible for precipitating adverse effects.

It is impossible, either before or after the induction of a hypnotic trance, to ascertain if a subject is likely to adversely react to a therapy. In addition, and of some importance, any adverse reaction to a therapy is not due to the negligent or careless manner in which the therapy is applied, because the ill effects arise naturally in any event. However, even though arising naturally, the frequency of serious adverse psychological effects arising upon the application of therapies must be examined. The reason is to support, or otherwise, the question of whether a clinical hypnotiser should reasonably foresee a risk of injury to the subject.

There are three studies examined in Chapter 5 that include relevant data from clinical settings, but the bases of collection varies between the studies and as a result cannot be combined to provide significant statistical evidence of frequency.

Based upon the evidence of infrequency of serious psychological ill effects arising upon the application of therapies it is clear that the risk is so small, if not minuscule, that a hypnotiser could not reasonably foresee that injury could be caused to a subject. This must be the situation even in the unlikely event of a hypnotiser being aware of the risk. Lord Reid, in the *Bolton v Stone*, case referred to man not creating '[…] a risk which is substantial'. The risk taken upon applying therapies is, of course, most insubstantial.

In the same case of *Bolton v Stone* the matter of taking precautions was raised with the rules established in that case being applied in the matter of injury arising from the non-termination of a hypnotic trance. It was entirely appropriate when discussing nontermination to take into account what, if any, precautions could be taken to guard against the risks. The reason is because in Lord Oaksey's judgement, quoted earlier, in *Bolton v Stone* he stated that precautions are to be taken against '[…] risks which are reasonably likely to happen'. It is, however, a completely different matter concerning serious adverse psychological effects arising from the application of therapies, because the risks are 'not likely to happen'. The question of taking precautions, if indeed any can be taken, is thereby not relevant in the clinical context.

A therapeutic hypnotiser is not in breach of a duty to achieve a reasonable standard of care and thereby not liable to a subject who suffers injury even though of a serious psychological nature.

Damage

The third element constituting the tort of negligence is damage. The meaning of damage is simply loss or harm to a plaintiff and within the context of this chapter means harm (i.e. injury) to the subject caused by a hypnotiser.

In a civil action for damages (i.e. financial compensation) it must be shown that the subject suffered damage as a result of negligence on the part of the hypnotiser. Throughout this chapter, based upon the law of negligence applicable to the negligent hypnotist, the injuries being sought and qualifying as damage to the subject, are those of 'serious adverse psychological effects'. For the same reasons in both criminal and civil assault discussed earlier in this book (see sub-subheading of 'The nature of psychological injury in assault' in Chapter 4) both minor and transient adverse psychological effects in negligence are discounted. This means that ordinary everyday complaints such as headaches, dizziness and transient feelings of anxiety and depression are not of any real interest in the tort of negligence.

When assessing if damage to the plaintiff is actionable in negligence the courts do not directly refer to DSM-IV, but there is a strong inference that the 'serious psychiatric damage', invariably mentioned in negligence cases, is that of the types listed in DSM-IV. On the other hand the courts have frequently disallowed damage which they regard as a minor or temporary nature of which some adverse effects are mentioned above and, of course, do not appear in DSM-IV.

The law relating to serious psychiatric damage is equally applicable to the tort of negligence as well as in both civil and criminal assault.

Pre-existing Conditions and Negligence

A 'pre-existing condition'. This term means either a physical, or mental, ailment that existed prior to the induction of a hypnotic trance and which was not caused by induction, or subsequent hypnotic procedures.

Danger of precipitating a mental disorder

The case of *Gates v McKenna* provides the answer as to whether a pre-existing, although latent, mental disorder can be precipitated, or triggered, by the induction of hypnosis. Gates, the plaintiff, developed schizophrenia shortly after participating in a stage show conducted by McKenna, the hypnotist defendant, for which he blamed the allegedly negligent McKenna. The judge, Mr Justice Toulson, stated in his judgement that there were two reasons why the action must fail:

> First, I do not consider that the defendant had reason to foresee a risk of the plaintiff suffering from schizophrenia [...] from the experience. [...] I am not persuaded that that it was reasonably foreseeable that an adult in apparent good health would have been at risk of suffering anything more than possible transient upset or discomfort from the experience, as distinct from physical or mental illness. [...] Second, the defendant failed to do, or did, anything which a reasonably careful exponent of stage hypnotism ought to have done or omitted.

This judgement is a good example of a court applying the by then well established rules pertaining to the law of negligence and set out earlier in this chapter. Applying the rules to this case one can say that because there was no reasonably foreseeable risk of Gates suffering serious adverse psychological effects there was no duty upon McKenna to give a precautionary warning against taking such a risk. He was, of course, found not responsible to Gates in damages, because he had not acted negligently towards him.

Danger of making an existing condition worse

This danger contemplates the substitution of an adverse medical condition with one that is more serious. Examples are provided by Rosen and Barterneier (1961) and other writers (see Chapter 4) of which one is an acute schizoid psychosis being substituted for a hypnotically cured numbness of the arm. In these circumstances there can be no doubt that the hypnotiser could not reasonably foresee this reaction in a subject and thereby not be liable in the law of negligence.

Danger of prolonging disorder

West and Deckert (1965) advise that there is only indirect and inferential evidence that disorders require a longer period of treatment by hypnotherapy than beyond the time when it would have considerably improved or even cured. There is no scientific proof of this danger and, therefore, it is discounted as a ground for an action in the tort of negligence.

Danger of superficial relief

An example of this danger is set out in Chapter 4 and relates how a hypnosis subject is successfully treated for what is assumed to be migraine pain, but the pain is actually caused by a tumour on the brain. In this circumstance the symptom is removed, but the root cause is allowed to progress undetected, and without treatment, much to the detriment of the subject's mental and physical health.

Even though the tumour was of organic origin it could be argued that the hypnotiser was responsible for additional injury to the subject, of the type listed in DSM-IV, because of non-detection of the progressive adverse medical condition. However, in practice these circumstances would rarely arise, and the degree of risk involved is minimal, a hypnotiser could not be said to be negligent upon not reasonably foreseeing and indeed diagnosing the danger.

To conclude this chapter upon the tort of negligence and the hypnotist one can confidently state that a hypnotist could only be found liable in damages to a subject in the event of not terminating the hypnotic trance properly and thoroughly, or making no attempt whatsoever to terminate.

Chapter 14

Australian Law

The major historical sources of Australian law are from the English legal system. It was extended and developed to, including custom (common law), the common law courts (creating case law) and legislation. In fact, Australian law can be traced back to the English Anglo-Saxon times with two of its categories being criminal and civil laws. The latter category includes the law relating to civil assault and negligence which are of particular interest in this chapter.

Even today the decisions of the English courts, whilst not binding upon the Australian courts, were stated in the Australian High Court case of *Cook v Cook* [1968] as being useful for their 'degree of persuasiveness of their reasoning'. In Australian court cases the most 'persuasive' decisions are understandably those emanating from the English House of Lords, the Court of Appeal and the High Court.

The Australian laws of criminal and civil assault, and the tort of negligence, are generally little different to the English law set out earlier in this guide. This particularly being the case in its applicability to injury arising out of the induction of a hypnotic trance and associated procedures.

Furthermore, in common with the UK and many other countries world wide, DSM-IV is accepted and used in medical circles throughout Australia.

However, despite these commonalties in the English and Australian laws of assault, negligence and DSM-IV listed serious psychological injury, it is still necessary to highlight the main points and also tease out any nuances that may exist regarding the legal liability of a hypnotiser operating in Australia.

Criminal Assault

It will be recalled that DSM-IV listed injuries can arise from the therapeutic use of hypnosis in a clinical setting and also, in all hypnotic settings, to certain cases of the non-termination of a trance.

To constitute criminal assault in each of these circumstances there present both an *actus reus* and a *mens rea* (see Chapter 10 for a full explanation). Professor David Barker, the Dean of the Faculty of Law at the University of Technology in Sydney, confirms that that almost all criminal offences require these two elements and quotes the Latin maxim: *Actus non facit reum nisi mens sit rea*, which means 'the act does not make him guilty unless the mind be guilty' (2000, p. 187).

While the *actus reus* is readily identifiable in most criminal activity it is sometimes not easy to decide if the element of *mens rea* is also present. *Mens rea* can be either subjective or objective. The subjective element refers to the state of mind of the accused as to what was actually thought at the time of the criminal act. The objective element test invokes a standard below which an accused fails to act, or think, as an ordinary person would in the same circumstances.

By far the majority of criminal offences apply the subjective test with the objective test being relevant only to the common law offence of manslaughter (based upon gross negligence) and strict liability, or absolute offences such as those relating to driving and food.

It is important to note that intention and recklessness are major constituent elements of the subjective *mens rea* requirements. Both elements, particularly that of recklessness, have a crucial role in deciding if a hypnotiser has committed a criminal assault, as it will be seen later in this chapter.

Intention as an element of mens rea is given its ordinary every day meaning by the courts as it was in the case of *R v Maloney* [1985] (see sub subheading of 'Intention' in Chapter 10) when Maloney tragically shot dead his father in law with a shot gun. Intention in this broad sense of the word can also include the concept of reck-lessness (*Vallance* [1961]).

The Australian Model Criminal Code states persons as intending to act if they mean to engage in that act and that they intend to bring about a consequence if they:

- mean to bring it about; or
- are aware that it will occur in the ordinary course of events (s. 203.1(Cth)).

The latter part of this section means that if a consequence is virtu-ally certain an accused is deemed to have intended it even though he or she may not have wanted it.

Similes for intention used by judges in both the English and Australian courts are: 'wanting', 'wishing', 'aiming at' and 'desiring'.

Recklessness as an element of *mens rea* is generally used in the sub-jective sense of the word in that it is the unreasonable and unjusti-fiable taking of a risk which is known by the accused. Recklessness, therefore, differs from intention which is the knowledge possessed by an accused when it is known, or it is virtually certain, that a par-ticular consequence will follow. Thus, a person is reckless about something when it is known, or foreseen as a possible consequence.

In *R v Crabbe* [1985], an indifference to risk was discounted as an element of recklessness when the court held:

> It is not the offender's indifference to the consequences of his act but his knowledge that those consequences will probably occur that is the relevant element.

This is an important aspect of recklessness as part of *mens rea* which becomes very evident when considering serious psycholog-ical injury arising from criminal assault.

When investigating serious psychological adverse effects associ-ated with the dangers of hypnosis earlier in this guide it was decided that they only arose upon two occasions. First, the application of therapies and secondly, when a hypnotic trance was not properly and thoroughly terminated, or no attempt whatsoever was made to terminate. Naturally this is the case world wide.

Neither intention, nor recklessness, as elements of *mens rea* were present in the application of therapies. There could be no intention present – as part of *mens rea* – when a therapy was being applied because the purpose of the hypnotic procedure was to improve the subject's health and not to cause serious adverse psychological effects. Furthermore, and of great importance, the likelihood of injury arising is so remote that there can be no evidence of intention on the part of the hypnotist.

However, it was a different matter when applying the law relating to recklessness, as an element of mens rea, where adverse effects arose as a result of the trance not being properly and thoroughly terminated by the hypnotist, or no attempt whatsoever being made to terminate. Recklessness as a state of mind must be present when a hypnotiser, in any settings, fails to terminate a trance. The hypnotiser must foresee, or be deemed to foresee, that a lack of the hypnotic termination procedure could be a risk leading to serious psychological adverse effects.

In the circumstances of non-termination the legal requirement of the *actus reus* and *mens rea* both being present at the same time (called the 'coincidence') is satisfied upon the induction of the hypnotic trance. At that time the hypnotiser must have foreseen, or be deemed to have foreseen, the risk that could arise upon failure to terminate the trance.

Even though the above interpretation of the law relating to *actus reus* and *mens rea* clearly applies to the nontermination of a trance one must now examine the Australian law of criminal assault to ascertain if an offence can be thereby committed.

The Federal Government does not have a general power to make criminal law in Australia because it is restricted in that regard under the constitution. It is therefore left to each of the seven states to enact its own criminal law with the country administratively divided into four separate jurisdictions. However, despite this division there is little, or no difference between the criminal laws of each state, and the law of assault can be generally applied throughout the country.

In common with English law there are four offences of criminal assault in Australia and each can be related to like offences in the other country. It is interesting to note that the Australian offences often rely upon English case law for interpretation.

The least serious of the criminal assaults is that of common assault for which the penalty is prescribed in legislation, but the offence itself continues to be defined at common law. Common assault at English law is still an offence at common law even though it is also contrary to Section 39 of the Criminal Justice Act 1988. The other three Australian criminal assault offences are comprehensively contained in statute law.

Historically, common assault in Australia distinguished between assault and battery, but this distinction no longer applies. The current concept of common assault incorporates the historical offences of psychic assault, whereby a defendant puts his victim in fear of imminent physical force and, in addition, the application of unlawful physical force upon the victim. In practice the defendant will be charged purely with assault, whether he has committed a psychic assault, a battery or both.

Where physical force is used by an accused the *actus reus* of common assault is readily understandable, but where the accused commits a purely psychic assault (i.e. no physical contact with the victim) the courts must rely on case law. There are many court precedents where it has been held that the absence of a positive act can satisfy the *actus reus* element of common assault, provided the accused behaves in a way as to induce a fear in the victim that he is about to be physically harmed. It has even been held that a threat over the telephone constitutes a positive act on the part of the accused (*Barton v Armstrong* [1969]), so long as the threat produces a fear or apprehension of physical violence, although the victim does not know when the violence will take place.

The *mens rea* of common assault relies upon either the element of intent, or recklessness. The only danger of serious psychological injury likely to be caused to a hypnotic subject is that of failure to properly and thoroughly terminate the trance, or the hypnotiser making no attempt whatsoever to terminate. Intent as an element of *mens rea* was not appropriate to this danger of hypnosis, but recklessness as an element was certainly applicable. Therefore, an accused commits an offence of common assault when he indulges in reckless conduct that could give the victim reasonable grounds for supposing that the accused intends to inflict harm upon him, or actually does harms him.

The offence of common assault requires the accused to be possibly, and not probably, aware of harm that could be caused to the victim. Case law supports this possibility of harm in, for example, the South Australian case of *MacPherson v Brown* [1975] when it was stressed that an accused must subjectively recognise his reckless behaviour:

> [...] Not by his actual intention, knowledge or foresight, but by what a reasonable prudent man would have intended, known or foreseen in the circumstances. (Bray CJ at page 188.)

This case implicitly admits recklessness as a form of *mens rea*, which is entirely compatible with harm, or injury caused by a hypnotiser not properly and thoroughly terminating a hypnotic trance, or making no effort whatsoever to do so.

There is one other ingredient to complete the offence of common assault where adverse effects or injury (called 'harm' in the definition) arise from from the non-termination of a hypnotic trance and that is whether the injury is envisaged by the offence.

The only harm discussed in this guide emanates from the psychic assault moiety of the offence where the accused creates an apprehension of imminent unlawful physical contact. The type of injury envisaged is certainly not DSM-IV listed and would include, for example, short-lived hysterical reaction (not the hysteria listed under the main heading of 'personality Disorders' in DSM-IV set out in Part I of Appendix B (p. 191)). In fact, any harm contemplated by the criminal offence of common assault would be minor, transient and emotion related.

After common assault the next most serious form of assault is that of 'assault occasioning actual bodily harm' (ABH) with the equivalent in English law being called the same and contrary to Section 47 of the Offences Against the Person Act 1861 (OAP Act).

This offence is the same as common assault, but happens to additionally cause bodily harm so the *mens rea* is identical to common assault (*R v Coulter* [1988]). This means that the subjective test of recklessness is again appropriate. However, the nature of the injury envisaged by ABH must be considered to ascertain if it completes the offence by being DSM-IV listed.

As long ago as 1934 in the case *R v Donovan* ABH was defined as including:

> [...] Any hurt or injury calculated to interfere with the health or comfort of the victim, such hurt or injury need not be permanent, but must, no doubt, be more than merely transient or trifling. (P. 509.)

When dealing with a Section 47 of the OAP Act, bruising is a good example of ABH. Importantly the court in held in *R v Miller* [1954] as there is no requirement of permanence of injury, but an injury that results in the victim suffering shock, or 'any psychiatric injury' may amount to an assault occasioning actual bodily harm. This case, and many others subsequently, admitted psychiatric harm to the offence of ABH and also, by implication, to all other criminal assault offences. However, in the ABH offences the psychiatric injury which is contemplated is clearly not of a sufficiently serious nature such as to be found in DSM-IV. The serious adverse psychological effects arising from nontermination of a hypnotic trance, due to the reckless conduct by a hypnotiser, are not to be found in the offence of assault occasioning actual bodily harm.

In the hierarchy of the seriousness of criminal assault offences the next most serious is that of what is simply labelled 'wounding'. Even though the statutory offence of wounding is identical in all respects throughout Australia it is variously referred in different jurisdictions as 'intentionally wound' (Australian Capital Territory), 'maliciously wound' (New South Wales and South Australia), 'unlawfully and maliciously wound' (South Australia again) and 'causing serious injury' (Victoria).

As mentioned earlier the *mens rea* requirement for all assault offences is satisfied by the element of recklessness and as a result the non-termination of a trance, in the circumstances earlier prescribed, is recognised by this more serious offence of wounding.

Next to be considered in relation to the criminal offence of wounding is whether the type of injury envisaged is of a nature that would satisfy the DSM-IV test adopted in this book. It was stated in *R v Vallance* [1961] that a wound is an injury which breaks through the whole skin, that is, both the inner and outer skin and with this type of wound including serious, deep knife wounds. This sort of injury is far more serious than the earlier discussed ABH which itself was more serious than the initially considered common assault. Wounding is the stage at which DSM-IV listed injury is admitted to assault offences.

The wounding offence is mirrored in the equivalent offence at English law of Section 20 OAP Act. The case of *R v Miller* included 'any psychiatric injury' as part of the ABH offence, but it was expressed to be injury not of a permanence and therefore, being of a minor or transient nature, did not encompass any of the more serious DSM-IV listed psychiatric disorders. However the offence of wounding is obviously a different matter and most certainly recognises DSM-IV listed disorders.

The final type of assault, and the most serious, to be considered is the offence to cause or inflict grievous bodily harm upon a person (GBH). The most important word in this definition is 'cause'. It has been held that there is no requirement of direct, or indirect application of force, provided the accused is shown to be responsible for the GBH. This is an ideal situation when contending that DSM-IV listed injury has been caused by a hypnotiser not properly, or thoroughly terminating a hypnotic trance, or not making any effort to do so.

In English law the main difference between the most serious of all assaults, being GBH with intent, which is contrary to Section 18 OAP Act and Section 20 is that of intent. However, in the Australian offence of GBH intent is not the overriding issue in that recklessness, as a form of *mens rea*, is admitted in like manner to the other three types of assault discussed.

In so far as injury is concerned the nature required for a GBH offence is in the most serious form imaginable and was defined as 'really serious bodily injury' in the case of *R v Perks* [1986]. Serious injury in this regard included the victim's skull being fractured or strangulation to the point of unconsciousness. In addition GBH injury has been defined by statute (in New South Wales and Australian Capital Territories) as 'any permanent or serious disfiguring of the person'. There is no real difference in injuries between Section 20 and Section 18 of the OAP Act, but there is a difference between the Australian wounding and GBH offences in that the latter is of a more serious nature.

Serious psychological effects listed in DSM-IV qualify as injury in both the wounding and GBH assaults unlike common assault and ABH.

Next, the consent of the hypnotic subject to the induction of the hypnotic trance and associated procedures providing a defence to the hypnotist who criminally causes DSM-IV listed injuries to arise should be considered. These serious injuries for which the hypnotist is responsible in criminal law are restricted to those arising as a result of the omission to terminate a hypnotic trance.

In English law, a person cannot consent to the infliction of serious injury (i.e. ABH and wounding), including DSM-IV listed disorders, upon himself or herself. These were not the sort of injuries of the nature where either implied consent (e.g. a handshake, accidentally bumping into someone in a crowded street and in sporting events), or express consent (e.g. tattooing and body piercing) were appropriate in the hypnotic context. Similarly, informed consent which is restricted to certain medically oriented situations.

The position is identical in Australian law where the courts specifically refer to cases such as the House of Lords case of *R v Brown and other appeals* [1994] where both the accused persons and the victims practised sado-masochistic pastimes with consensual serious injury being inflicted upon each other. The accused were convicted of both ABH and wounding despite the victims readily providing their consent. In any event it is illogical for a subject to be able to consent to the infliction of serious psychological harm, in any of the hypnotic settings, where he, or she is unaware of the risk and not able to quantify it.

Civil Assault

Anita Stuhmcke, a senior lecturer in law at Sydney's University of Technology, defines trespass to the person (i.e. assault and battery) at civil law as:

> Trespass to the person means that any unwanted or unjustified interference with a person's body, liberty or a creation of fear of such interference is actionable at law. (2001, p. 79)

It can be seen from this definition that the tort of what is commonly referred to as 'assault' is again divided between an assault and a battery.

The latter part of the definition contains the assault moiety of the civil wrongdoing and refers to 'a creation of fear'. Stuhmcke (2001, p. 81) enlarges upon this creation of fear by further describing it as 'an apprehension of imminent harmful or offensive contact'. This is clearly not applicable to the circumstances of adverse psychological effects arising from either the application of therapies, or upon a hypnotiser's default regarding the nontermination of a trance. Irrespective of the hypnotic setting a hypnotiser could never be accused of an 'unwarranted or unjustified [...] creation of fear' in a subject. In any event it is impossible in these circumstances to perceive serious adverse psychological effects of the type listed in DSM-IV being caused. Therefore, this leaves the 'battery' part of the definition to be examined where DSM-IV listed injury arises when the hypnotiser applies a therapy, or does not terminate a trance.

Once again, we can rely upon Stuhmcke for a fuller definition of battery when she writes:

> A battery is a direct and intentional act of the defendant which has the effect of causing contact with the body of the claimant without their consent.

It can be readily seen that a battery is committed by a defendant when physical force is used and also when it is an intentional and voluntary act.

The two circumstances of serious adverse effects being caused by the application of therapies and by the hypnotiser not properly and thoroughly terminating a trance, or making no effort to do so, are most above certainly not contemplated by the battery element of civil assault. There is a lack of physical force, no contact with the body of the subject and the unintentional and involuntary nature of the hypnotist's conduct.

So, there is no point in continuing the examination of civil assault and hypnosis at Australian law. It is, however, interesting to note that in English law the situation, regarding civil assault and the responsibility of a hypnotist upon causing injury to a subject, is exactly the same in that no liability is incurred.

Consent as a defence to civil assault is not a concept to be considered, because civil assault is not applicable to injury arising from hypnosis. This does not mean that a hypnotist is not liable to a subject in the tort of negligence.

Negligence

If an English lawyer were to be asked what was the most important, and well known, case in civil law the answer would be invariably be the 1932 English Appeal Court case of *Donoghue v Stevenson*. The same question posed of an Australian lawyer would produce the same answer. This case is the basis of the law of negligence in both countries and even today, some seventy years later, the principles established in *Donoghue v Stevenson* continue to apply.

In accordance with these principles, in an action based on the defendant's negligent behaviour, the claimant has to establish the defendant owes him a duty of care, the defendant is in breach of that duty of care and he, the claimant, has suffered damage arising from the breach. The elements in Australian law fully match English law. (See Chapter 13).

The first element to be considered is duty of care which is a legal requirement establishing a link between the claimant and defendant. After Donoghue Stevenson this link became known as the 'neighbour test' which refers to the Lord Atkin judgement and the reasonable foreseeability of the risk of harm to the claimant. Unlike the subjective test in criminal assault mentioned earlier the neighbour test is objective, that is, what a reasonable person would have foreseen in the same situation. Therefore, there is a duty of care where there is a foreseeable risk of injury to others if reasonable care is not taken. These 'others' are regarded as Lord Atkin's neighbours, which is a concept often referred to in the Australian courts as 'proximity'. This is clearly a situation which embraces the hypnotist and subject relationship.

To maintain a successful civil action for negligence the claimant must demonstrate that the defendant is in breach of a duty of care, which is the second element of the tort of negligence. The law has again generally adopted the objective test, or standard of what 'a reasonable person of ordinary prudence' would have done in the same circumstances. This is the 'Mr Average', or the 'man on the Clapham omnibus' test in English law.

The standard of care determined by the court is resolved by it considering whether a reasonable person in the defendant's position would have foreseen that the conduct posed a risk of injury to the claimant reasonableness of the defendant's response to the risk.

In determining this objective standard of care the court may take into account what it considers to be relevant factors. Most relevant to the hypnotiser and subject relationship is the factor of the likelihood of injury arising. It was clear from the detailed examination of the serious adverse effects caused by the application of therapies that they were relatively unknown. This perhaps goes some way to ruling out any liability attaching to a hypnotiser in the therapeutic setting. However, this might not apply to the other danger of hypnosis of a hypnotiser's failure to properly and thoroughly terminate the trance, or making no effort whatsoever to terminate. In these circumstances the research clearly shows that the risk of serious psychological injury is not only very real, but also greater than upon the application of therapies.

In the High Court case of *Nagle v Rottnest Island Board* [1993] it was stated: '[…] A risk may constitute a foreseeable risk even though it is unlikely to occur […] It is enough that the risk is not far-fetched or fanciful.'

Subsequently, it has been held, for example, that damage caused by oil catching fire on Sydney Harbour was a reasonably foreseeable risk, as it was not far-fetched or fanciful. It must therefore be accepted that the risks associated with the application of therapies, and non-termination of a trance, are both foreseeable.

However, if the likelihood of harm arising and the seriousness of the risk and injury are combined with two other relevant factors of 'use of the defendant's acts' and 'practicability of precautions' there can be no doubt that serious injury arising from the two circumstances of non-termination is due to the hypnotiser's negligence. Conversely, these two additional factors must completely exculpate the clinical hypnotherapist from liability to the subject in the tort of negligence.

The 'use of the defendant's acts' factor simply means the social benefit to be derived from the hypnosis. The courts treat the greater the social utility of the defendant's acts as greater the evidence of the behaviour being reasonable. This factor must operate in favour of the hypnotherapist, but certainly not where a hypnotist has negligently defaulted in respect of termination of the hypnotic trance.

The practicability of the taking precautions by the hypnotiser refers to those precautions which the operator could take to avert harm to the defendant. Amongst the practicalities of taking precautions a court would take into account are the expense and inconvenience of eliminating the risk. Upon the non-termination of the trance due to the hypnotiser's default a court would undoubtedly take the view that it would cost nothing and not be inconvenient for the hypnotiser to terminate. It follows that the hypnotiser must be liable in negligence to the subject in respect of any serious psychological adverse effects which may arise.

Moreover, where a hypnotist holds himself out as having special hypnotic skills an even higher standard of care is expected.

The matter of special skills, the relevant factors and the foresee-ability of a risk of injury in determining the standard of care and its breach, of which aspects of the tort of negligence are equally appli-cable in both English and Australian law.

The final element of the tort of negligence is that of damage. In the present context damage, harm or injury means those adverse psychological effects listed in DSM-IV and arising from hypnotic procedures.

Any serious psychological DSM-IV listed adverse effects arising from the application of therapies is not due to the negligence of the hypnotiser, but that can not be said of the hypnotiser who fails to properly and thoroughly terminate a hypnotic trance, or makes no effort to do so.

Finally, the reader is reminded that negligence is based upon an unintentional, or careless act by the defendant, whereas assault requires an intentional act (see subheading of 'Assault and battery' in Chapter 11). For a defence of consent to be successful the defen-dant must show that the claimant agreed to an actual event taking place. It follows that the very nature of a negligent act, being unin-tentional and, no doubt, unexpected by the claimant, precludes the defence of consent.

It is concluded that the liability of a hypnotiser in Australian law is restricted to that of criminal assault and civil negligence, only in respect of the default in terminating a hypnotic trance, which is identical to liability incurred in English law.

Chapter 15

American Law

It speaks well of the validity of English common law and case law that they continue to the present day to greatly influence the laws of America, even though it declared its independence from England as long ago as 1776.

Throughout its colonisation America was subject to the English common law, which goes back to the Norman Conquest of 1066.

After independence, the new American states adopted the English common law with its judges greatly relying on Blackstone's Commentaries of 1769. These commentaries were written by Sir William Blackstone who codified the principles of English common law. In due course much of the common law (particularly criminal offences) was largely embodied in state statutes, but the American courts even today still rely upon the common law for definition and case law for interpretation. Some variations were introduced in the legislation to incorporate the new social and political environment, but in general American and English criminal and civil laws are so very similar.

In both English and Australian law if an injury is listed in DSM-IV it is a serious injury, which qualifies as an element of illegal assault at both criminal and civil law and, also, in the tort of negligence. If the injury was not listed in DSM-IV (i.e. being of a minor or transient nature) it can be discounted. Assaults and negligence transgressions not included in DSM-IV are incomplete and consequently the hypnotiser is not responsible.

DSM-IV is compiled and published by the American Psychiatric Association and naturally it is accepted and relied upon throughout America in all medical circles.

Criminal Assault

In common with both English and Australian criminal law the elements of a crime in America are, *actus reus* (a wrongful act), *mens rea* (a guilty mind) and the accused has no defence to the crime with which he, or she is charged. If an accused has a valid defence, such as consent in a criminal assault charge, or there is neither *actus reus*, nor *mens rea* present, then no convictable offence has been committed. Furthermore, the *actus reus* and *mens rea* must both occur concurrently (called 'concurrence').

One can look to the criminal case of *State v Quick* to see how *actus reus* and *mens rea* operate in practice. Quick was heading towards his property, where he kept all the paraphernalia for making illegal liquor. In his vehicle he had the ingredients for making the liquor, which the law officers discovered after stopping him. He was charged and subsequently convicted of unlawfully making liquor. The conviction was reversed on appeal on the basis that the intent (*mens rea*) to manufacture illegal liquor was not accompanied by a concurrent and overt and voluntary physical (*actus reus*).

When a DSM-IV-listed injury arises from hypnosis, even at the end of the hypnotic session when failing to dehypnotise, the concurrence of the *actus reus* and *mens rea* occurred upon the induction of the trance. The voluntary physical act, comprising the *actus reus*, is satisfied by the exercise or movement of those parts of the body enabling the hypnotiser to speak in pursuance of the induction of a hypnotic trance.

The *actus reus* of the induction of the trance is a fairly easy concept to understand, but that is not entirely the case with *mens rea*. Before undertaking an examination of *mens rea* the reader is reminded of the two circumstances where serious psychological injury may arise in connection with hypnosis. The first such circumstance is upon the application of a hypnotic therapy and the other when the hypnotiser fails to thoroughly and properly terminate the hypnotic trance, or makes no effort whatsoever to do so. The former takes place in the clinical setting and the latter in all settings.

The somewhat complicated question of intent, recklessness and negligence as forms of *mens rea* have already been discussed in connection with criminal assault at both English and Australian law. American criminal law applicable to the same concepts is much simpler.

Mens rea is often described as 'criminal intent' in the sense of a person having a guilty mind. This can be misleading because there are a number of interpretations of the term guilty mind. For example, in the case of *In re Hayes* the court observed, '[...] An essential element of every orthodox crime is a wrongful or blameworthy state of mind.'. The word 'blameworthy' extends the terms of criminal intent, or guilty mind, in a subjective manner, which can be clearly seen upon an analysis of the Model Penal Code (MPC). This code was drawn up in 1962 by the American Law Institute, a body comprising prominent lawyers, judges and academics. Whilst some courts have applied the MPC others still cling to the common law terms for intent, but of both applications should be considered particularly as intent, or other blameworthy conduct, is at the heart of criminal assault.

The MPC proposes four states of mind (*mens rea*): Purposeful, knowing, reckless and negligent acts. The purposeful act is defined as one taken with an intent to cause a particular result. A knowing act is one taken when the result is practically certain to occur. Neither of these definitions is compatible with the state of mind of a hypnotiser when serious psychological injury (i.e. DSM-IV listed) is caused to a subject. The induction of a hypnotic trance and associated procedures – such as the application of therapies – are not undertaken by a hypnotist with the intent to cause injury, or knowing that injury is certain to occur. However, it is a different matter in respect of the other two MPC definitions of the state of mind. A reckless act as one taken in disregard of a substantial risk. A negligent act as one taken by a person who fails to perceive the substantial risk of harm that may result from it. There can be no doubt that both these states of mind, as forms of *mens rea*, could apply to a hypnotiser who does not thoroughly and properly terminate a hypnotic trance, or makes no effort whatsoever to do so and, as a result, serious psychological injury is caused. Injury arising from a therapeutic application, whilst under hypnosis, is not within either the reckless, or negligent state of mind, because the risk of injury is so remote and also such risk is unlikely to be within the knowledge of the hypnotiser.

Other than when applying the MPC, the courts follow the common law classification of specific and general intent, mainly because the law is based on precedents created in other cases, even though the criminal offence is contained in a statute.

General intent can best be described by reference to *Myers v State* when the Indiana appellate court stated: General intent exists when from the circumstances the prohibited result may reasonably be expected to follow from the offender's voluntary act, irrespective of a subjective desire to have accomplished such result.

As with the MPC, the injury arising from the failure to dehypnotise is envisaged by general intent, but not DSM-IV listed injury caused by hypnotically applied therapies.

Specific intent is not applicable because that it requires the offender to specifically intend the particular result that occurs.

An assault is committed by a person intentionally causing another to fear an immediate battery, whereas a battery is generally defined as an intentional bodily injury upon another.

American law, in common with English and Australian law, distinguishes between an assault and battery, but assault is invariably used as a generic term to describe both assault and battery.

While both England and Australia have four separate statutory offences of assault depending on the seriousness of the injury (see Chapters 10 and 14) American law recognises only one. The assault can be aggravated by, for example, the offending party being intent to commit a more serious crime, or by the means to perpetrate the assault such as using a deadly weapon.

Some years ago in English law the two general categories of misdemeanours and felonies were abolished, but they continue to be part of the American legal system. A simple assault falls into the descriptive category of a misdemeanour, but the more serious offence of aggravated assault is classified as a felony, where the penalties are normally much more severe. During the induction of a hypnotic trance, and the application of associated procedures, the hypnotiser does not intended to commit a more serious crime, nor can hypnosis be regarded as a deadly weapon. Therefore, even though serious psychological harm can be caused by the hypnotiser's failure to dehypnotise, any assault thereby occasioned is a misdemeanour.

To convict a defendant of the misdemeanour of simple assault the prosecution have to prove the act, the defendant's intent and the injury. The act (*actus reus*) is the induction of the hypnotic trance combined with the failure to thoroughly and properly terminate it, or making no effort whatsoever to do so. If the MPC is being applied by the court the intent (*mens rea*) is either that of recklessness, or negligence. The hypnotiser has either recklessly disregarded the substantial risk of psychological harm arising upon failure to dehypnotise, or failed to perceive the risk.

Upon the trial of person charged with assault the court may follow the older general intent basis of *mens rea*. In that regard the court, in a hypnosis based offence of assault, would undoubtedly decide that intent exists because the hypnotist should have reasonably expected the psychological harm to arise from the induction of the trance and subsequent failure to dehypnotise.

The American criminal law applicable to *mens rea* and assault were much simpler than in English and Australian law, in that there is only one offence of assault to be considered and there are no real complications regarding proof of the accused's state of mind (*mens rea*).

The final ingredient of criminal assault to be considered is that of the interpretation of the term 'bodily harm' taken from the earlier definition of battery.

In like manner to criminal assault in English law it has long been established in the American criminal courts that mental harm (called psychiatric or psychological injury in English law) is admitted to assault offences. Naturally the harm must be of a serious nature (such as those listed in DSM-IV) to qualify as so-called 'bodily harm'. Moreover, the mental harm must not be transient, or of a common every day nature (e.g. headache, dizziness and nausea).

To secure a conviction the accused must be unable to produce a valid defence. Consent is a defence that may be available to an accused charged with assault.

Historically, the American courts have said that consent is not a defence to assault because the victim may not excuse a criminal act. However, this statement does not necessarily exclude, either the defence of implied consent, or informed consent. For the purpose of this guide the law in America can be regarded as identical to that of both English and Australian law. The reasonableness of physical force is the test in sporting contests, such as football and boxing, when a defence of implied consent is appropriate. Likewise being accidentally jostled in a crowd. Consent is also a good defence for medically qualified persons who perform bodily invasive procedures having first fully informed the patient about the procedure, and any risks, to which they are to be subjected.

A hypnotic subject is unable to consent to the infliction of serious psychological harm in any hypnotic settings. This must particularly be the case because the subject is unaware of any risk and, as a result, is unable to quantify it.

Civil Assault

Edward J. Kionka (1999, p. 149), a professor of law at Illinois University, advises that the tort of battery is '[...] an intentional and unpermitted physical contact with plaintiff's person by defendant by an agency the defendant has set in motion'.

This definition echoes the definition of civil assault (battery) in Halisbury's Laws of England at English law and Anita Stuhmcke in Australian law. The reader is reminded that there were two reasons why no liability attached to the hypnotiser, even upon serious psychological harm being caused to a subject, however it may arise. The same two reasons are applicable in American. The lack of *physical* force upon the part of the hypnotist and, the *unintentional* and involuntary nature of the hypnotist's conduct.

The reference by Kionka to 'unpermitted' physical contact invokes the concept of the lack of consent from the plaintiff in allowing the assault to be committed by the defendant. This matter of consent in civil assault is not applicable to injury arising from hypnosis.

Negligence

To fully set out the American law of negligence would be to repeat the same basic English law in Chapter 13 and in Chapter 14 concerning Australian law.

In all three countries the premise of the tort of negligence can be described as every person being under a duty, at all times, to behave in a manner so as not to create unreasonable risk of harm to others.

Arising from this description there are three major components of the tort. They are, first, a duty of care is owed by the defendant to the plaintiff, secondly, the defendant is in breach of that duty of care by failing to conform to a reasonable standard of conduct and, finally, the plaintiff has suffered loss or damage caused by the defendant's breach of duty of care. An easy way to understand the tort of negligence is to regard it as importing the absence of carefulness as a state of mind, which implies forgetfulness, or inattention on the part of the defendant. To a lawyer, of course, it is not that simple.

To establish that a duty of care is owed by the hypnotiser to the subject, an objective test must be applied. This test asks if a reasonable person would have foreseen the risk of injury in the same situation if reasonable care is not taken. A duty of care must exist if only for the reason that psychological injury, arising by virtue of the hypnotiser failing to dehypnotise the subject, should have been foreseeable by any reasonable person. The reasonable person is the previously mentioned Mr Average.

The second component is that of the hypnotiser being in breach of the duty of care and the reasonableness of the response to the foreseeable risk. In the hypnotiser and subject relationship the response to the foreseeable risk is unreasonable if the hypnotiser fails to thoroughly and properly terminate the hypnotic trance, or makes no effort whatsoever to do so. This is clearly negligent conduct particularly as it would be known to the hypnotiser, and most certainly foreseeable, that failure to dehypnotise was risky and could result in psychological harm to the subject. The hypnotiser would be further condemned in the eyes of a court if the risk could have been simply avoided by a properly administered termination procedure, which would be at a nil cost to the hypnotiser. On the other hand the risk of injury arising from the danger of the application of therapies is not only so remote as to be highly unlikely to occur, but is most unlikely to be known to hypnotist. As a result it cannot be said that in law the hypnotist was negligent.

The final component of negligence in the hypnotic setting is damage (in the sense of adverse psychological injury or harm) caused by the hypnotiser to the subject arising from a breach of duty of care. Both physical, and so-called mental harm by the American courts, qualify as elements of this final component. Mental distress, ranging from depression through neuroses and psychoses, is harm upon which a plaintiff may rely to successfully claim damages (monetary compensation) from a negligent defendant. Such a claim is not restricted to negligence claims, but is available in all civil law actions. Naturally, the plaintiff subject must prove that the hypnotist defendant caused serious adverse psychological effects by the negligent failure to thoroughly and properly terminate the hypnotic trance, or that no attempt whatsoever was made to do so.

DSM-IV is an excellent benchmark to apply to ascertain if adverse psychological effects are of a sufficiently serious nature to qualify as mental harm in a negligence action. By this means any unlisted DSM-IV ordinary, or transient every day complaints, for example, headache, dizziness, nausea and also emotions such as unhappiness and embarrassment can be eliminated.

The matter of consent to an act of negligence operating as a defence is negated by Kionka (1999, p. 133) when he writes, '[...] Assumption of risk is plaintiff's voluntary consent to encounter a known danger created by defendant's negligence.' The 'known danger' arising from failure to dehypnotise only occurs as a result of the hypnotiser's carelessness, or inattention to dehypnotise. This is not something that is 'known' prior to induction of the trance and, therefore, the unintentional nontermination of the trance must exclude consent as a form of defence.

Chapter 16

Key Conclusions for Good Practice

Principal Conclusions

- The induction of a hypnotic trance is not an illegal assault on the mind. There cannot be an illegal assault (in the sense of committing a criminal offence or being liable for damages in civil law) without, having caused serious injury of the nature listed in the current Diagnostic and Statistical Manual of Mental Disorders (DSM-IV). Hypnosis *per se* not associated with adverse psychological effects of the descriptions listed in DSM-IV.

- The application of hypnotic therapies can produce serious psychological adverse effects which are listed in DSM-IV. However, no criminal offence of assault is committed, in the absence of all forms of *mens rea*. Furthermore, in civil law no liability is incurred, because it is a requirement that not only is the *actus reus* a physical act, but also contact be made with the victim. The same situation exists at both Australian and American law.

- In certain circumstances the non-termination of a hypnotic trance can amount to a criminal offence of assault. The two circumstances concern the hypnotiser not properly and thoroughly terminating the hypnotic trance, or not making any effort whatsoever to terminate. Adverse effects arising from the circumstances of nontermination can amount to serious injury satisfying the 'bodily harm' requirement of Sections 47 and 20 of the Offences Against the Person Act 1861, provided they are listed in DSM-IV. Again the same circumstances amount to criminal assault in both Australia and America.

- The same two circumstances of non-termination do not create any liability to the hypnotiser in the tort of trespass to the person (assault) at either English, Australian and American civil law. An action for damages in respect of an unintentional act is in the tort of negligence, with civil assault only recognising intentional acts as a form of *mens rea*.

- Hypnosis is not, and cannot be, one of the exceptions to the general rule that a person is not able to consent to the infliction of serious injury upon himself, or herself, at both criminal and civil law. In criminal law the main reason a subject cannot consent to the hypnotiser not terminating the trance, in the two circumstances mentioned earlier, is that assault requires intent as the *mens rea*, whereas nontermination involves recklessness. Nontermination does not create any liability in assault at civil law and, therefore, it follows that consent is irrelevant. The English law relating to all forms of consent is functionally identical to that of Australia and America.

- Informed consent cannot apply to the induction of a hypnotic trance and other hypnotic procedures because, among other things, it does not involve surgery or invasive tests.

- A hypnotiser can only be liable in the tort of negligence upon the failure to terminate the hypnotic trance resulting in DSM-IV listed injury to the subject. Unlike DSM-IV listed injury arising upon the application of therapies, where the risk is so small it is not reasonably foreseeable by the hypnotiser. As a result a hypnotiser in a therapeutic setting incurs no liability in the law of negligence. It was decided that the English principles of law concerning the tort of negligence are equally applicable in both Australia and America.

- Even though there is no consensus upon the nature of hypnosis – not even amongst the experts – it was decided in this guide that expert evidence upon the characteristics of the hypnotic trance is likely to acceptable to the English courts and also in the Australian and American courts.

Appendix A

Part I – Permissive Method Induction Script

(Eye Fixation with Progressive Relaxation)

Sit back comfortably in the chair. Choose a spot on the ceiling, slightly behind. Look up and backwards at it ... OK. Now keep your eyes fixed on that spot on the ceiling. Let yourself go limp ... and slack ... let all the muscles of your body relax completely. Breath quietly ... in ... and out. Now I want you to concentrate upon your feet and ankles, let them relax ... let them go limp and slack ... you will begin to notice that your feet are feeling heavy. As though your feet are becoming as heavy as lead ... feeling as though they are sinking into the carpet. Keep your eyes fixed on that spot on the ceiling ... and as you stare at it you will find that your eyelids are becoming heavier and heavier ... so that presently they will want to close. As soon as they feel they want to close ... just let them close. Let yourself go completely. Let the muscles in your calves and thighs go quite limp and relaxed ... let them relax ... let them go limp and slack. And as they do your eyes are beginning to feel more and more tired ... more and more tired . They are becoming a little watery. Soon, they will feel so heavy that they will want to close. As soon as they feel they want to close ... just let them close entirely on their own. Let the tension go completely ... give yourself up totally to this very ... very pleasant ... relaxed drowsy ... comfortable feeling. Let your whole body go limp and slack ... heavy as lead. Now, the muscles in your stomach ... let them relax ... let them go limp and slack ... now the muscles in your chest ... and your back ... feeling limp and slack and very ... very relaxed ... letting them relax completely. And as you can experience a feeling of heaviness in your body. As though your whole body is becoming just as heavy as lead. As if it is wanting to press down ... deeper and deeper ... into the chair. Just let your body go as heavy as lead. Let it sink back comfortably ... deeper and deeper into the chair.

And as it does so ... your eyelids are feeling even heavier and heavier. So very, very heavy that they are wanting to close. And now, that feeling of relaxation is spreading into the muscles of your hands and arms your shoulders and neck. Let your neck muscles relax ... let them go limp and slack ... let them relax completely. And as they do so ... you will notice a feeling of heaviness in your hands and arms ... as if they are becoming as heavy as lead. Let them relax completely. And the heaviness spreads pleasantly and comfortably through your neck and facial muscles to your eyes and eyelids. And as it does ... so your eyelids are feeling very ... very tired and very ... very ... heavy ... your eyes are feeling very, very, heavy ... very ... very tired ... that they are wanting to close. Wanting to close, now ... closing ... closing ... relaxed and pleasant feelings of tension leaving your body, and with your body relaxing more and more. Your eyes are wanting to close, ... now ... closing ... closing tighter and tighter.

Go to sleep!

Part II – Intermediate Method Induction Script

(Erickson's Hand Levitation Method)

I want you to sit comfortably, and let yourself relax. Place your hands palms downward upon your thighs. Fix your eyes upon your hands ... and keep watching them ... very, very closely. And whilst you are relaxing like this ... you will notice certain things are happening ... that you had not noticed before. I will point them out to you. Now, I want you to concentrate upon all the sensations and feelings that you notice in your hands ... no matter what they might be. It may be that you will feel the texture of the material of your trousers/skirt as your hands rest on your thighs. You may feel the warmth of your hands on your thighs ... or you may feel a certain amount of tingling of your hands. No matter what your sensations may be ... I want you to observe them closely. Keep watching your hands. They seem to be quite still ... resting in one position ... yet some movement is there ... although it is not yet noticeable. Keep watching your hands. Don't let your attention wander from them. Just wait to see what movement is going to show itself.

It will be interesting to see which of your fingers moves first. It may be any finger ... or it may even be your thumb. But one of the fingers is going to twitch or move. You don't know which one or even in which hand. Neither do I ... but keep watching ... and you will find that one of them will move.. Possibly in your right hand. See! The thumb twitched and moved ... just as I said. And now you will notice that a very interesting thing is beginning to happen. You will notice that the spaces between your fingers are gradually beginning to widen. The fingers will move slowly apart ... and you will see that the spaces will become wider and wider. Your fingers are slowly moving apart ... wider ... wider ... wider ... wider. The spaces are becoming wider ... wider ... wider ... wider.

Now, I want you to watch carefully what is taking place. Your fingers will want to rise up slowly from your thigh ... as if they want to lift up ... higher ... higher ... and higher. You see! Already your forefinger is beginning to lift up. As it does so ... all the other fingers will want to follow. (The other fingers begin to rise).

As the other fingers lift ... your entire hand is beginning to feel lighter and lighter. So light ... that your whole hand will slowly rise in the air ... as if it feels just as light as a feather ... just like a feather. As if a balloon is slowly lifting it up in the air. Lifting ... lifting ... up ... and up ... and up. Pulling it up ... higher ... higher ... higher. Your hand is becoming lighter and lighter ... very, very light indeed. (The hand starts to rise).

As you watch your hand rise ... you will notice that your entire arm is beginning to feel lighter and lighter. It is wanting to rise in the air ... as if it feels just as light as a feather. As if a balloon is slowly lifting it up in the air. Lifting ... lifting ... up ... and up ... and up. Pulling it up ... higher ... higher ... higher. Your hand is becoming lighter ... very, very light indeed. (The hand starts to rise).

As you watch your hand rise ... you will notice that your entire arm is beginning to feel lighter and lighter. It is wanting to rise up in the air . notice how your arm is lifting up in the air ... up ... and up ... and up ... a little higher ... and higher. (The arm has lifted about 6 inches above the thigh, and the subject is gazing at it intently.)

Keep watching your hand and arm ... as it slowly rises into the air. And as it does so ... you will begin to feel drowsy and tired. Notice how drowsy and tired your eyes are becoming. As your arm continues to rise ... you will feel more ... and more tired and relaxed ... very, very sleepy ... very, very sleepy indeed. Your eyes will become heavier and heavier ... and your eyelids will want to close. As your arm rises ... higher and higher ... you will want to feel more and more relaxed. You will want to enjoy this very, very pleasant ... relaxed ... sleepy feeling Just let yourself go ... give yourself up entirely to this very, very comfortable ... relaxed ... drowsy feeling.

Your arm is lifting up ... and up ... and up ... and up. Higher ... higher ... and higher. And you are feeling very, very drowsy indeed. Your eyelids are becoming heavier ... and ... heavier. Your breathing is becoming slower ... and deeper. Breath slowly and deeply ... in ... and out ... in ... and out.

As you keep watching your hand and your arm ... you are feeling more and more drowsy ... and relaxed. And now you will notice that your hand is changing direction. The elbow is beginning to bend ... and your hand is beginning to move ... closer and closer to your face. Your hand is moving ... slowly but surely ... towards your face. And as it becomes closer and closer ... you are feeling drowsier and drowsier ... and you will fall into a deep sleep. Closer and closer ... drowsier and drowsier ... sleepier and sleepier. Although you are becoming sleepier and sleepier ... you must not go to sleep until your hand touches your face. But when your hand touches your face ... you will fall immediately into a deep, deep sleep.

Your hand is now changing direction. It is moving closer and closer to your face. Your eyelids are feeling heavier and heavier. You are becoming ... sleepier and sleepier ... and sleepier. Your eyelids are becoming heavier ... and heavier. Your hand is moving closer and closer to your face. You are becoming drowsier ... and drowsier ... more and more tired. Your eyes are wanting to close now ... closing ... closing. When your hand touches your face ... they will close immediately. You will fall into a very, very deep sleep. Drowsier ... and drowsier ... very, very sleepy ... very, very tired. Your eyelids are beginning to feel as heavy as lead. Your hand is moving closer and closer to your face. Closer ... and closer ... closer to your face. The moment it touches your face ... you will fall into a very, very deep sleep. (The subject's hand touches his/her face, and the eyes close).

Go to sleep Go to sleep Sleep very, very deeply And as you sleep ... you will feel very, very tired ... and relaxed. Let yourself go ... let yourself relax completely. Think of nothing but sleep ... deep, deep sleep.

Part III – Authoritarian Method Induction Script

(Further Modified Elman Technique)

Now ... just rest back comfortably and take a deep breath. As you breath out, close your eyes. Now let your entire body relax from your head to your toes and as you do so your eyes close tighter and tighter. As your eyes close tighter your body relaxes more and more. As you relax more and more your eyes close tighter and tighter. As all the muscles of your eyes relax more and more, your body relaxes more and more. In fact the muscles of your eyes are so relaxed that you just can't be bothered to use them. Don't use them. Let them relax more and more - more and more. You can't be bothered to use them. Good - very good. Now when I count from one to three your eyes will open and then from three to one and they will close again and you will double the feeling of relaxation - - - one, two, three - eyes open - three, two, one - eyes closed and deeply relaxed, deep, deep, deeply relaxed.

If the subject's eyes open other than after the above count of three, then the following procedure can be adopted:

Good ... good ... good ... now let them close again and double the feeling of relaxation. Very, very relaxed ... all the way around your eyes. Your eyelids, your eyeball and every single muscle that controls the movement of your eyes. Just let go of any remaining tension ... completely relaxed. Relax more and more, relax your eyes more and more. So much so that the muscles will not want to work. Let them relax more and more so that you temporarily put them out of action and they won't work, they just don't want to. Open your eyes. Good ... good ... good ... now really open them and close them again and double the feeling of relaxation. *(Process can be repeated over and over until the subject eventually follows the instructions.)*

Now your entire body relaxes ... all your facial muscles, your chin and jaw muscles ... down through the muscles in your neck to your shoulders and shoulder joints. Your shoulder blades and every bone and joint in your spine, every muscle and nerve in your back. From your shoulders down each arm and hand to your fingertips and from your shoulders through your chest and stomach muscles and down to the tips of your toes ... all completely relaxed.

(What follows is part of the induction, but also works as a deepener.) Now I want you to see the number 100 in your mind ... see it in front of you. In a moment I will ask you to count backwards from 100, all in your mind, but when you lose track of the numbers, or cannot be bothered to concentrate anymore, I want you to raise the first finger on your right hand, I repeat when you lose track of the numbers, or cannot be bothered to concentrate anymore, I want you to raise the first finger of your right hand. Now, focus your attention on the number 100 in your imagination and with each number you count backwards your feeling of relaxation will double ... deeper and deeper into relaxation. I will count the first three numbers with you. Now, start to slowly count backwards ... ninety nine ... deeper and deeper ... ninety eight ... deeper and deeper ... . Let the numbers just fade away ... and deeper ... deeper. Ninety seven ... deep ... deep ... deep ... . Can't be bothered to count anymore ... . The numbers are fading away ... let the numbers fade away ... . Can't be bothered ... deeply, deeply, deeply relaxed ... . Go to sleep *(It is permissible, after a long silence, to repeat the IMR (Ideo Motor Response) instructions i.e. raising the finger – and if there is still no response it can be assumed that a trance has been induced).*

Part IV – Deepener by Imagery Script

(On holiday)

I would like you to imagine a situation in which you are on holiday. You are staying in a beautiful resort where the sun always shines and the temperature is just as you like it. You spend part of the day relaxing and part of it, if you wish, exploring or in more active occupations. This is the relaxing part. Just wander down to the gardens, and look around at the peaceful scene before you. Note the mass of exotic plants and vivid colours of the flowers. Take a deep breath ... and as you breath out relax deeper and deeper. Wander slowly towards them and as you approach them the scent is more fragrant than any you have experienced. Take a deep breath again and inhale the soft, warm and perfumed air ... and as you breath out, relax deeper and deeper. Now continue on your way, to that pretty winding pathway which takes you down to the beach. Wander along, relaxing deeper and deeper with every step. There is that beach with miles of golden sand. There, a sunshade especially for you and beneath it a most inviting deck chair. Stroll across the sand to the chair, sit down, slip off your shoes and just lie back. Adjust the sun shade so that it is just right for you ... Take a deep breath once more and relax deeper and deeper as you breath out. Look out at the calm blue sea, the waves are lapping lazily on the beach and a fishing boat, with its colourful sail, is bobbing up and down. The sun is shining, the sky is blue and not a cloud is in sight ... Take a deep breath, and as you breath out relax deeper and deeper than ever before ... and as you relax deeper and deeper ... Go to sleep ... sleep ... deep, deep, sleep ... deeper and deeper than ever before.

Part V – Termination Script

In a few moments ... when I count to seven ... you will open your eyes and feel wide awake again. You will wake up feeling wonderfully better for this deep, relaxing sleep. You will feel completely relaxed ... both mentally and physically ... quite calm and composed ... without the slightest feeling of drowsiness or tiredness. Next time ... you will not only be able to go into this sleep much more quickly and easily ... but you will be able to relax very much deeper. Each time, in fact ... your sleep will become deeper and deeper. One, you are thinking of wakening ... two, you are becoming awake ... three, you will soon be wide awake and alert ... four, you are returning to full consciousness ... five, you are coming back to a full conscious waking state ... six, you are at – ** – and the time is – ** – in the – ** – ... seven, **eyes open ... wide awake and alert**.

Part VI – Lecron and Bordeau System for Defining Depths of Trance

Depth	Symptoms and phenomena exhibited
Insusceptible	Subjects fail to react in any way
Hypnoidal	Physical relaxation Drowsiness apparent Fluttering of eyelids Closing of eyes Mental relaxation, partial lethargy of mind Heaviness of limbs
Light trance	Catalepsy of eyes Partial limb catalepsy Inhibition of small muscle groups Slower and deeper breathing, slower pulse Strong lassitude (disinclined to move, speak, think or act) Twitching of mouth or jaw during induction Rapport between subject and operator Simple post-hypnotic suggestions heeded Involuntary start or eye twitch on awakening Personality changes Feeling of heaviness throughout entire body Partial feeling of detachment
Medium trance	Recognition of trance by subject Complete muscular inhibitions Partial amnesia Glove anaesthesia Tactile illusions Gustatory illusions

Olfactory illusions
Complete catalepsy of limbs or body

Deep or Ability to open eyes without affecting trance
somnambulistic Fixed stare when eyes are open; pupillary dilation
Somnambulism
Complete amnesia
Systemized post-hypnotic amnesias
Complete anaesthesia
Post-hypnotic anaesthesia
Bizarre post-hypnotic suggestions heeded
Uncontrolled movements of eyeballs; eye
co-ordination
Sensation of lightness, floating, swinging, of
being bloated or swollen; detached feeling
Rigidity and lag in muscular movements and
reactions
Recurring variation in loudness of operator's
voice
Control of organic body functions (heartbeat,
blood pressure, digestion and so on)
Recall of lost memories (hyperamnesia)
Age regression
Positive visual hallucinations, post-hypnotic
Negative visual hallucinations, post-hypnotic
Positive auditory hallucinations, post-hypnotic
Negative auditory hallucinations, post hypnotic
Stimulation of dreams (in trance or post-
hypnotic in natural sleep)
Hyperaesthesia
Colour sensations experienced

Plenary trance Stuporous condition in which all spontaneous
activity is inhibited. Somnambulism can be
developed by suggestion to that effect.

Appendix B

Part I – Major Categories in DSM-IV

(From Diagnostic and Statistical Manual of Mental Disorders of 1994)

Delirium, dementia, amnestic and cognitive disorders: dementia's (e.g. of Alzheimer's type); amnestic disorders.

Schizophrenic and other psychotic disorders: schizophrenia (paranoid, disorganised, catatonic, undifferentiated and residual types); schizophrenic disorder; schizoaffective disorder.

Substance-related disorders: alcohol-use disorders; hallucinogen-use disorders; opiod-use disorders; sedative, hypnotic or anxiolytic substance-disorders.

Mood disorders: depressive disorders (e.g. major depressive disorder); bipolar disorders (e.g. bipolar I disorder, such as a single manic episode, and bipolar II disorder, i.e. recurrent major depressive episodes with hypomania); cyclothymic disorder.

Anxiety disorders: panic disorder (with or without agoraphobia); agoraphobia; specific or simple phobia; social phobia; obsessive-compulsive disorder; post-traumatic stress disorder.

Somatoform disorders: somatisation disorder; conversion disorder; hypochondriasis.

Dissociative disorders: dissociative disorder; dissociative fugue; dissociative identity disorder or multiple personality disorder; depersonalisation disorder.

Adjustment disorders: adjustment disorder (with anxiety, depressed mood, disturbance of conduct, mixed disturbance of emotions and conduct, or mixed anxiety and depressed mood).

Disorders first diagnosed in infancy, childhood or adolescence: mental retardation (mild, moderate, severe, profound); learning disorders (reading disorder, mathematic disorder, disorder of written expression); disruption-behaviour and attention deficit disorders (attention deficit/hyperactivity disorder).

Personality disorders: paranoid; schizoid; schizotypal; antisocial; borderline; histrionic; narcissistic; avoidant; dependent; obsessive-compulsive.

Sexual and gender identity disorders: sexual desire disorders; sexual arousal disorders; paraphilias (e.g. exhibitionism, fetishism, voyeurism); gender identity disorders (in children, adolescents or adults).

Impulse control disorders not elsewhere classified: intermittent explosive disorder; kleptomania; pyromania; pathological gambling.

Factitious disorders: factitious disorder with predominantly psychological or physical signs and symptoms.

Sleep disorders: dyssomnias (e.g. primary insomnia, narcolepsy); parasomnias (e.g. sleep terror disorder, sleepwalking disorder).

Eating disorders: anorexia nervosa; bulimia nervosa.

Mental disorders due to a general medical condition not elsewhere classified: catatonic disorder due to a general medical condition; personality change due to a general medical condition.

Other conditions that may be a focus of clinical attention: rational problems; problems related to abuse or neglect; additional problems that may be a focus of clinical attention (e.g. bereavement, occupational problem, phase of life problem).

Part II – MacHovec's List of Complications Associated with Hypnosis

anergia
antisocial acting out
anxiety, panic attacks
attention deficit
body/self-image distortions
comprehension/concentration loss
confusion
coping skills impaired
decompensation, psychotic-like
delusional thinking
depersonalization
depression
derealization
dizziness
dreams
drowsiness, excessive sleep
fainting
fear or fearlessness
guilt
headache
histrionic reactions
identity crisis
insomnia

memory impaired, distorted
misunderstood suggestion
nausea, vomiting
obsessive ruminations
overdependency
personality change
phobic aversion
physical discomfort, injury
psychomotor retardation
psychosis
regressed behaviors
sexual acting out
sexual dysfunction
somatization
spontaneous trance
stiffness, arm or neck
stress, lowered threshold
stupor
symptom substitution
tactile hallucinations
traumatic recall
tremors
weeping, uncontrolled

Bibliography

Books

American Psychiatric Association (1994) *Diagnostic and statistical manual, Revised (DSM-IV)*, Washington DC, American Psychiatric Press.

Bemheim, H. (1886/1973) *Hypnosis and suggestion in psychotherapy*, New York, John Aronson.

Braid, J. (1843) *Neurypnology: Or the rationale of nervous sleep considered in relation with animal magnetism*, London, Churchill.

Bruer, J. and Freud, S. (1955) 'Studies on hysteria', in *Complete Works of Sigmund Freud*, (ed Strachey), Vol.11, pp. 1893–1895, London, Hogood Press.

Card, R., Cross, and Jones (1998) *Criminal Law*, London, Butterworths.

Chemnitz, G, and Feingold, E. (1980) 'Various conditions of suggestion and suggestibility and their significance for medical and psychotherapeutic treatment, in Pajntar, Roskar and Lauric (eds), *Hypnosis in Psychotherapy* and *Psychosomatic Medicine*, Ljubjana, University Press.

Clarkson, C.M.V. and Keating, H.M. (1998) *Criminal Law: Text and Materials*, London, Sweet & Maxwell.

Estabrooks, G.H. (1957) *Hypnotism*, New York, Dutton.

Esdaile, J. *(1846) Mesmerism in India and its practical application in surgery* and *medicine*, London, Longmans.

Eysenck, H.J. (1970) The *Structure of Human Personality*, London, Methuen.

Gibson, H.B. and Heap, M. (1991) *Hypnosis in Therapy*, Hove, England, Lawrence Erlbaum.

Gill, M.M. and Brenman, M. (1959) *Hypnosis and Related States*, New York, International Universities Press.

Halisbury's Laws of England (1985) fourth edition, editor Lord Hailsham of Marylebone, vol.45, London, Butterworths.

Hilgard, E.R. (1965) *Hypnotic Susceptibility*, New York, Brace & World.

Hilgard, E.R. (1978) 'States of consciousness in hypnosis: divisions or levels?' in *Hypnosis at its Bicentennial'* (eds Frankel and Zamansky), New York, Plenum.

Hilgard, E.R. (1986) *Divided consciousness: Multiple controls in human thought and action*, New York, Wiley.

Hilgard, J.R. (1970) *Personality and hypnosis: A study in imagination involvement*, Chicago, University of Chicago Press.

Hilgard, E.R. (1991) 'A Neodissociation Interpretation of Hypnosis', in Lynn, S.J. and Rhue, J.W. (eds) *Theories of Hypnosis: Current Models and Perspectives*, New York, Guildford Press, pp. 83–105.

Hull, C.L. (1933) *Hypnosis and suggestibility: An experimental approach*, New York, Appleton Century Crofts.

Jones, M.A. (1998) *Textbook on Torts*, sixth edition, London, Blackstone Press.

Karle, H.W.A. (1991) 'Professional and ethical issues' in Heap, M. and Dryden, W. (eds) *Hypnotherapy: A Handbook*, Milton Keynes, Open University Press, pp. 184–199.

Lynn, S.J. and Rhue, J.W. (1991) 'An Integrated Model of Hypnosis' in Lynn, S.J. and Rhue, J.W. (eds) *Theories of Hypnosis: Current Models and Perspectives*, New York, Guildford Press, pp. 397–438.

MacHovec, F.J. (1986) *Hypnosis Complications*, Springfield Illinois, Charles C. Thomas.

Martin, E.A. (ed) (1994) *A Dictionary of Law*, Oxford, Oxford University Press.

McGill, O. (1947) The *Encyclopedia of Stage Hypnotism*, Calon, Mich., Abbots Magic Novelty Co.

McGill, O. (1996) The *New Encylopedia of Stage Hypnotism*, Carmarthen, Wales, Anglo American Book Company.

Orne, M.T. (1972) 'On the simulating subject as a quasi-control group in hypnosis research: What, why and how? in E. Fromm & R.E. Shor (eds) *Hypnosis: Research Developments and Perspectives*, Chicago, Aldine-Atherton, pp.399–443.

Oxford Concise Medical Dictionary (1998) Martin, E.A. (ed), fifth edition, Oxford, Oxford University Press.

Percy, R.A. (1990) *Charlesworth & Percy on Negligence*, London, Sweet and Maxwell.

Reber, A.S. (1995) *Dictionary of Psychology*, London, Penguin Group.

Shor, R.E. and Orne, E.C. (1962) *Harvard Group Scale of Hypnotic Susceptibility, Form A*, Palo Alto, California, Consulting Psychologists Press.

Scheflin, A.W. and Shapiro, J.L (1989) *Trance on Trial*, New York, The Guildford Press.

Shor, R.E. (1969) 'Hypnosis and the concept of the generalised reality-orientation', In *Altered States of Consciousness*, (ed Tart), New York, Anchor Doubleday.

Spanos, N.P. (1991) 'A Sociocognitive Approach to Hypnosis', in Lynn, S.J. and Rhue, J.W. (eds) *Theories of Hypnosis: Current Models* and *Perspectives*, New York, Guildford Press, pp.324–361.

Thornton, E.M. (1976) *Hypnotism, hysteria, and epilepsy: An historical synthesis*, London, Heinemann.

Wagstaff, G.F. (1996) 'Compliance and imagination in hypnosis', in Kunzendorf, R.G., Spanos, N.P. and Wallace, B. (eds), *Hypnosis and Imagination*, (pp.19–40), New York, Baywood, pp.19–40.

Waxman, D. (1981) *Hypnosis*, London, Unwin Paperbacks.

Waxman, D. (1989) *Hartland's Medical and Dental Hypnosis*, London, Bailliere Tindall.

Weitzenhoffer, A.M. and Hilgard, E.R. (1959) *Stanford Hypnotic Susceptibility Scale, Form C*, Palo Alto, California, Consulting Psychologists Press.

Wolpe, J. (1958) *Psychotherapy by Reciprocal Inhibition*, Stanford California, Stanford University Press.

Journal Articles

Auerback, A. (1962) 'Attitudes of Psychiatrists to the Use of Hypnosis', *Journal of the American Medical Association*, 11, 917–921.

Barber, T.X. (1961) 'Antisocial and Criminal Acts Induced by Hypnosis', *Archives of General Psychiatry*, 5, 109–120.

Barber, T.X. (1969) 'An Empirically-based Formulation of Hypnotism', *American Journal of Clinical Hypnosis*, 12, 100–130.

British Medical Association (1955) Report from Psychological Medicine Group Sub-committee, *British Medical Journal (Suppl.)*, 1, pp. 190–193.

Chaves, J.F. (1997) 'The State of the "State" Debate in Hypnosis', *International Journal of Clinical* and *Experimental Hypnosis*, 3, 251–265.

Coe, W.C. (1973) 'Experimental Designs and the State-Nonstate Issue in Hypnosis', *The American Journal of Clinical and Experimental Hypnosis*, 16, 118–128.

Coe, W.C. (1992) 'Hypnosis: Wherefore art thou?', *The International Journal of Clinical and Experimental Hypnosis*, 4, 219–237.

Coe, W.C. and Ryken, K. (1979) 'Hypnosis and Risks to Human Subjects', *American Psychologist*, 8, 673–681.

Conn, J.H. (1972) 'Is hypnosis really dangerous?', The *International Journal of Clinical* and *Experimental Hypnosis*, 2, 61–79.

Conn, J.H. (1981) 'The myth of coercion through hypnosis: A brief communication', The *International Journal of Clinical and Experimental Hypnosis*, 2, 95–100.

Crawford, H.J., Hilgard, J.H. and MacDonald, H. (1982) 'Transient experiences following hypnotic testing and special termination procedures', The *International Journal of Clinical and Experimental Hypnosis*, 2, 117–126.

Danto, B.L (1967) 'Management of Unresolved Hypnotic Trances as Forms of Acute Psychiatric Emergencies', *American Journal of Psychiatry*, 124: 96–99.

Echterling, L.G. (1988) 'Contrasting Stage and Clinical Hypnosis', *American Journal of Clinical Hypnosis*, 4, 276–284.

Echterling, L.G.. and Emmerling, D.A. (1987) 'Impact of Stage Hypnosis', *American Journal of Clinical Hypnosis*, 3, 149–154.

Faw, V., Sellers, D.J. and Wilcox, W.W. (1968) 'Pathological effects of hypnosis', The *International Journal of Clinical and Experimental Hypnosis*, 1, 26.

Heap, M. (1995) 'A case of Death Following Stage Hypnosis: Analysis and Implications', *Contemporary Hypnosis*, 12, 99–110.
Heap, M. (1996) 'The Nature of Hypnosis', The *Psychologist*, 499-500.

Hilgard, E.R. (1969) 'Altered States of Awareness', *Journal of Nervous and Mental Diseases*, 149, 68–79.

Hilgard, E.R. (1973) 'A neodissociation interpretation of pain reduction in hypnosis', *Psychological Review*, 5, 396–411.

Hilgard, E.R. (1973) 'The domain of hypnosis: With some on alternative paradigms', *American Psychologist*, 28, 972–982.

Hilgard, J.R. (1974) 'Sequelae to Hypnosis', *International' Journal of Clinical and Experimental Hypnosis*, 22, 282–298.

Hilgard, E.R. (1977) 'The problem of divided consciousness: A neodissociation interpretation', *Annals New York Academy of Sciences*, 296, 48–59.

Hilgard, J.R., Hilgard, E.R. and Newman, M. (1961) 'Sequelae to Hypnotic Induction with Special Reference to Earlier Chemical Anaesthesia', *Journal of Nervous Mental Diseases*, 133, 461–478.

Hilgard, E.R. and Tart, C.T. (1966) 'Responsiveness to suggestibility following waking and imagination instructions and following induction of hypnosis', *Journal of Abnormal Psychology*, 3, 196–208.

Hodge, J.R. (1974) 'What Patients May Ask About Hypnosis', *Medical Times*, 1, 123–133.

Judd, K.J., Burrows, G.D. and Dennerstein, L. (1986) 'Clinicians' perceptions of the adverse effects of hypnosis: A preliminary survey', *Australian Journal of Clinical and Experimental Hypnosis*, 1, 49–60.

Kirsch, I. (1994) 'Defining Hypnosis for the Public', *Contemporary Hypnosis*, 3, 142–143.

Kirsch, I. and Lynn, S.J. (1995) 'The altered state of hypnosis: Changes in the theoretical landscape,' *American Psychologist*, 50, 846–858.

Kirsch, I., Mobayed, C.P., Council, J.R. and Kenny, D.A. (1972) 'Expert judgments of hypnosis from subjective state reports', *Journal of Abnormal Psychology*, 4, 657–662.

Kleinhauz M. and Beran, M.A. (1981) 'Misuses of hypnosis: A medical emergency and its treatment, The *International Journal of Clinical and Experimental Hypnosis*, 2, 148–160.

Kleinhauz, M. and Beran, M.A. (1984) 'Misuse of Hypnosis: A Factor in Psychopathology', *American Journal of Clinical Hypnosis*, 3, 283–290.

Kleinhauz, M., Dreyfuss, D.A., Beran, B., Goldberg, T. and Azikri, D. (1979) 'Some after effects of stage hypnosis: A case study of psychopathological manifestations', *The International Journal of Clinical and Experimental Hypnosis*, 3, 219–226.

Kleinhauz, M. and Eli, I. (1987) 'Potential Effects of Hypnosis in the Clinical Setting', *American Journal of Clinical Hypnosis*, 3, 155–159.

Klemperer, E. (1967) 'The Nature of Hypnosis', *Journal of the American Society of Psychosomatic Dentistry and Medicine*, 14, 49–54.

Kline, M.V. (1972) 'The production of antisocial behavior through hypnosis: New clinical data', The *International Journal of Clinical and Experimental* Hypnosis, 2, 80–94.

Kost, P.F. (1965) 'Dangers of Hypnosis', *The International Journal of Clinical and Experimental Hypnosis*, 4, 220–225.

Levitt, E.E. and Hershman, S. (1962) 'The Clinical Practice of Hypnosis in the United States: A Preliminary Survey', *International Journal of Clinical and Experimental Hypnosis*, 1, 55–65.

Lynn, S.J. (1997) 'Automaticity and Hypnosis', *The International Journal of Clinical and Experimental Hypnosis*, 3, 239–250.

Meeker, W.B. and Barber, T.X. (1971) 'Towards an explanation of stage hypnosis', *Journal of Abnormal Psychology*, 11, 61–70.

Meldman, M.J. (1960) 'Personality Decompensation After Hypnotic Symptom Suppression', *Journal of American Medical Association*, 173, 359–361.

Milgram, S. (1972) 'Some conditions of obedience and disobedience to authority', *Human Relations*, 18, 57–76.

Milne, G. (1986) 'Hypnotic compliance and other hazards', *Australian Journal of Clinical and Experimental Hypnosis*, 1, 15–29.

Orne, M.T. (1959) 'The Nature of Hypnosis: Artifact and Essence', *Journal of Abnormal Social Psychology*, 58, 277–299.

Orne, M.T. (1965) 'Undesirable effects of hypnosis: The determinants and management', *International Journal of Clinical and Experimental Hypnosis*, 4, 226–237.

Orne, M.T. (1972) 'Can a hypnotized subject be compelled to carry out otherwise unacceptable behaviour? *The International Journal of Clinical and Experimental Hypnosis*, 3, 101–117.

Orne, M.T. and Evans, F.J. (1965) 'Social control in the psychological experiment: Antisocial behavior and hypnosis', *Journal of Personality and Social Psychology*, 1, 189–200.

Orne, M.T., Sheehan, P.W. and Evans, F.J. (1968) 'Occurrence of posthypnotic behavior outside the experimental setting', *Journal of Personality and Social Psychology*, 2, 189–196.

Perry, C. (1977) 'Variables influencing the posthypnotic persistence of an uncanceled hypnotic suggestion', *Annals of New York Academy of Sciences*, 296: 264–73.

Perry, C. (1979) 'Hypnotic coercion and compliance to it: A review of evidence presented in a legal case', *The International Journal of Clinical and Experimental Hypnosis*, 3, 187–218.

Rosen, H. (1960) 'Hypnosis: Application and misapplication', *Journal of American Medical Association*, 172, 683–687.

Rosen, H. and Barthemeier, L.H. (1961) 'Hypnosis in Medical Practice', *Journal of American Medical Association*, 172, 976–979.

Sarbin, T. *(1950)* 'Contributions to role-taking theory: 1. Hypnotic behaviour', *Psychology* Review, 57, 255–270.

Sakata, K.l. (1968) 'Report on a case of failure to dehypnotise and subsequent reputed aftereffects', The *International Journal of Clinical and Experimental Hypnosis*, 4, 221–228.

Scott, D.L (1978) 'University training in medical and dental hypnosis', *Proceedings of the British Society of Medical and Dental Hypnosis*, Vol.4, No. 1, 13.

Spanos, N.P. and Barber, T.X., 'Towards a Convergence in Hypnosis Research', *American Psychologist*, 29, 7, 500–511.

Watkins, J.G. (1947) 'Anti-Social Compulsions Induced Under Hypnotic Trance', *Journal of Abnormal Social Psychology*, 42, 256.

Watkins, J.G. (1972) 'Antisocial behaviour under hypnosis: Possible or impossible?, *The International Journal of Clinical and Experimental Hypnosis*, 2, 95–100.

West, L.J. (1960) 'Psychophysiology of Hypnosis', *Journal of American Medical Association*, 172, 128-131.

West, L.J. and Deckert, G.H. (1965) 'Dangers of Hypnosis', *Journal of American Medical Association*, 192,95–98.

White, R.W. (1941) 'A preface to the theory of hypnotism', *Journal Abnormal Social Psychology*, 36, 477–505.

Williams, G.W. (1951) 'Difficulty in dehypnotising', *Journal of Clinical and Experimental Hypnosis*, 1, 3–12.

Table of Cases

Alcock *v* Chief Constable of South Yorkshire Police [1991] 4 All ER 907

Bolam *v* Friern Hospital Management Committee [1957] 1 W.L.R. 582

Bolton *v* Stone [1951] A.C. 850

Condon *v* Basi [1985] 2 All ER 453, CA

Chatterton *v* Gerson [1981] 1 All ER 257

Donoghue *v* Stevenson [1932] A.C. 562

Dorset Yacht Co. *v* Home Office [1970] AC 1004

Fowler *v* Lanning [1964] 2 All ER 929

Gates v McKenna [1998] 46 B.M.L.R. 9

Gold *v* Haringey Health Authority [1987] 2 All ER 888

Latimer *v* AEC Ltd [1953] AC 643

Letang *v* Cooper [1965] 1 QB 232, CA

MPC *v* Caldwell [1982] AC 341

Overseas Tankship (UK) Ltd *v* Miller Steamship Co. Pty Ltd

R *v* Burstow; Ireland [1997] Crim. L.R. 810, HL

R *v* Brown [1994] and other appeals 2 All ER 75, HL

R *v* Chan-Fook [1994] 2 All ER 552

R *v* Cunningham [1957] 2 QB 396

R *v* Hancock and Shankland [1986] AC 455

R *v* Lawrence [1982] AC 510

R *v* Miller [1954] 2 All ER 529

R *v* Moloney [1985] AC 905, HL

R *v* Savage [1992] 1 AC 699, HL

R *v* Spratt [1991] 2All ER 210, CA

R *v* Stephenson [1979] 1 QB 695

R *v* Wilson [1996] 2 Cr.App.R. 241, CA

Sidaway *v* Bethlem Royal Hospital Governors [1985] 1 All ER 643

Sidaway *v* Gerson [1985] 1 All ER 1018

Wells *v* Cooper [1958] 2 QB 265

Wilson *v* Pringle [1986] 2 All ER 440, CA

Index

Another title from
Crown House Publishing

Hypnosis and Counselling
in the Treatment of Chronic Illness
David Frank & Bernard Mooney PhD

This important work discusses the therapeutic properties of hypnosis in the treatment of life-threatening diseases. Including a brief history of hypnosis and an invaluable series of case studies, this work examines:

- The science of hypnosis
- Successful integration into the cancer treatment programme
- Myths surrounding the subject of hypnosis in therapy.

It raises questions about the direction medicine has taken and considers future developments. Presenting compelling arguments for offering hypnosis to cancer sufferers, this work provides crucial insight into the body's healing abilities – an insight of immense importance to medical professionals and everyone interested in the treatment and approach to diseases.

"This treatise is an easy read without obscure jargon or outrageous claims. It honestly alludes to the time, energy and skill required by the practitioner who wishes to use this modality of treatment. **It deserves to be on the reading list of medical personnel and their cancer patients.**"
– *K.L. Muth MD, FRCS, CRCS(C) – Surgeon*

David Frank is a published writer whose ten years experience of lecturing and counselling has seen him at further education colleges, medical centres, and general practitioner surgeries. He is a full member of The British Association for the Person Centred Approach, and The British Society for Clinical Hypnosis.

Bernard Mooney PhD is a qualified counsellor and lecturer, and has had over half a century of experience in teaching and counselling. He is a founder member of The British Association for the Person Centred Approach.

HARDBACK   160 PAGES   ISBN: 1899836748

USA & Canada *orders to:*

Crown House Publishing
P.O. Box 2223, Williston, VT 05495-2223, USA
Tel: 877-925-1213, Fax: 802-864-7626
E-mail: info@chpus.com
www.CHPUS.com

Australasia *orders to:*

Footprint Books Pty Ltd
4/92A Mona Vale Road, Mona Vale, NSW 2103, Australia
Tel: +61 (0)2 9997 3973, Fax: +61 (0)2 9997 3185
E-mail: sales@footprint.com.au
www.footprint.com.au

UK & Rest of World *orders to:*

The Anglo American Book Company Ltd
Crown Buildings, Bancyfelin, Carmarthen,
Wales, SA33 5ND, UK
Tel: +44 (0)1267 211880/211886, Fax: +44 (0)1267 211882
E-mail: books@anglo-american.co.uk
www.anglo-american.co.uk